AF322625

BREAKING THE CYCLE

Understanding and Escaping Financial Abuse

Babette Wilson

Author's Note

No part of this publication may be reproduced, stored in a retrieval system, or transmitted in any form or by any means, electronic, mechanical, photocopying, recording, scanning, or otherwise, without the prior written permission of the author.

This publication is designed to provide accurate and authoritative information in regards to the subject matter covered. It is sold with the understanding that neither the author nor the publisher is engaged in rendering legal, investment, accounting, or other professional services. While the author has used their best efforts in preparing this book, they make no representations or warranties with respect to the accuracy or completeness of the contents of this book and specifically disclaim any implied warranties of merchantability or fitness for a particular purpose. No warranty may be created or extended by sales representatives or written sales materials. The advice and strategies contained herein may not be suitable for your situation. You should consult with a professional when appropriate. The author shall not be liable for any loss of profit or any other commercial damages, including but not limited to special, incidental, consequential, personal, or other damages.

Cover design by: Freelance Contractor

This book is dedicated to all the survivors of financial abuse— the silent victims who have endured the invisible chains of control and manipulation. Your courage, resilience, and strength inspire us to fight for a future where financial freedom is a right, not a privilege. To those who have been silenced, this book is your voice.

Contents

Introduction

Financial abuse is often hidden in plain sight. It can be subtle, insidious, and manipulative, making it challenging for victims to recognize and address. This book delves into the dark underbelly of financial abuse, exposing the tactics used by abusers to gain control and exploit their victims. It challenges the misconception that financial abuse is a solely female issue, highlighting the devastating impact it has on both men and women.

"Breaking the Cycle" is more than just a book; it is a roadmap to freedom. It offers practical advice for navigating the emotional, psychological, and legal complexities of financial abuse. From recognizing the signs to developing a financial escape plan, this book provides a step-by-step guide for reclaiming financial independence and building a secure future.

This book is a testament to the strength and resilience of survivors. It celebrates their courage in breaking free from the chains of financial abuse and sharing their stories to empower others. It acknowledges the role of community, support systems, and professional help in overcoming the trauma of financial abuse. By shedding light on this often-overlooked form of domestic violence, "Breaking the Cycle" aims to spark a conversation, raise awareness, and foster a society that empowers individuals to break free from financial abuse and reclaim their rightful place in the world.

Preface

Financial abuse is a insidious form of domestic violence that often goes unnoticed, yet its impact can be devastating. It is a complex issue, weaving together the threads of control, manipulation, and isolation, leaving victims feeling trapped and powerless. While the subject may seem daunting, this book aims to provide a comprehensive and accessible guide for understanding, recognizing, and overcoming financial abuse.

This book is a beacon of hope for those seeking to break free from the cycle of financial abuse. It offers practical advice, empowering strategies, and real-life stories that illuminate the path to financial independence and freedom. Through a blend of personal narratives, expert insights, and actionable steps, "Breaking the Cycle" aims to equip readers with the knowledge and tools needed to reclaim their financial well-being and rebuild their lives.

CHAPTER ONE

The Hidden Face Of Domestic Violence

Financial abuse, often shrouded in secrecy and dismissed as a mere personal issue, stands as a stark reminder that domestic violence manifests in ways far more insidious than physical brutality. It seeps into the very fabric of a victim's life, entwining itself with their finances, isolating them from support, and chipping away at their self-worth. This invisible form of control, wielded through manipulation and coercion, leaves a trail of devastation, leaving victims trapped in a cycle of dependency and fear.

To grasp the true extent of financial abuse, we must first peel back the layers of societal norms that often downplay its severity. The insidious nature of this abuse often goes unnoticed, dismissed as simple arguments over finances or miscommunication. Yet, behind the façade of everyday disagreements lies a calculated strategy of control, where money becomes a weapon to silence, manipulate, and isolate.

Consider a woman, newly married and excited about starting her life with her partner. He controls the household finances, claiming to be better at managing money. At first, it seems practical, even helpful. But over time, she notices small changes: her access to joint accounts is limited, requests for spending money are met with scrutiny, and her credit cards are inexplicably denied. He dismisses her concerns as "being irrational" or "not understanding finances." He may even begin using her money without her consent, painting her as "incompetent" and needing his "guidance." This is financial abuse. He is wielding money as a weapon to control her, isolate her from support systems, and make her dependent upon him.

Financial abuse is not limited to romantic relationships. It can occur in families, with children, within friendships, and even within business partnerships. The common thread that unites all these instances is the abuser's desire to exert power and control over another individual through financial means.

It's crucial to recognize that financial abuse transcends mere financial hardship. It's not about a couple's inability to make ends meet; it's about one person deliberately using money as a tool to dominate and subjugate the other. This might involve tactics like withholding access to shared funds, preventing the victim from working or obtaining an education, forcing them into debt, or using their credit for the abuser's own personal gain.

The emotional toll of financial abuse is often overlooked. It can lead to feelings of helplessness, anxiety, fear, shame, and even depression. Victims may become increasingly withdrawn, struggling to maintain their independence and self-esteem. They may feel trapped, believing they have no way out of their situation.

The impact on victims can be devastating, extending far beyond the immediate financial consequences. It can hinder their ability to pursue education, secure stable employment, and build a secure future. It can also lead to social isolation, making it difficult to access support networks and escape the abusive relationship.

To further illustrate the hidden face of financial abuse, let's examine how it intersects with other forms of domestic violence:

Physical Abuse:

Often, physical violence is accompanied by financial abuse. The abuser may withhold money as punishment, or use financial control to prevent the victim from leaving or seeking help.

Emotional Abuse:

Financial abuse is often a tool for emotional manipulation. The abuser might use guilt trips, threats, and insults to control the victim's financial decisions. They might also belittle the victim's financial skills and make them feel dependent on them.

Sexual Abuse:

Financial abuse can create a power imbalance that facilitates sexual abuse. The abuser might use money as a means of controlling the victim's sexual activities or to force them into unwanted sexual encounters.

Psychological Abuse:

Financial abuse can have a profound impact on the victim's mental health. The constant stress, anxiety, and feeling of powerlessness can lead to depression, anxiety disorders, and even post-traumatic stress disorder.

Financial abuse doesn't always involve overt acts of violence. It can manifest through subtle forms of manipulation and control, making it difficult for victims to recognize they are being abused. This is precisely why it is crucial to understand the dynamics of financial abuse and its relationship to other forms of domestic violence.

Recognizing the signs of financial abuse is the first step towards breaking free. By understanding the tactics abusers employ and the emotional and psychological toll they inflict, we can empower victims to seek help and rebuild their lives.

It is time to shed light on the hidden face of domestic violence, acknowledging the devastating impact of financial abuse and providing support to those who have been victimized by it.

CHAPTER TWO

Recognizing The Signs Of Financial Abuse

Financial abuse can be a subtle and insidious form of control, often overlooked or dismissed as mere "money issues." But the truth is, financial abuse is a serious form of domestic violence that can have devastating consequences for victims, both emotionally and financially. It is a power play, a systematic attempt to strip victims of their autonomy and independence, leaving them trapped in a cycle of fear and dependence.

The abuser may use a variety of tactics to exert financial control, ranging from isolating the victim from their financial resources to making all financial decisions without their input. This could involve taking control of the victim's bank accounts, credit cards, or other financial assets, preventing them from accessing their own money, or forcing them to rely solely on the abuser for financial support.

Recognizing the signs of financial abuse can be the first step toward breaking free from this insidious form of control. Here are some common symptoms and red flags to watch out for:

1. Lack of Financial Transparency:

The abuser may be secretive about their finances, refusing to share information about their income, expenses, or investments. This lack of transparency is designed to keep the victim in the dark, making it difficult for them to understand the financial realities of the relationship and to identify any red flags.

2. Controlling Access to Money:

The abuser may limit or completely restrict the victim's access to their own money. This could involve taking control of their bank accounts, creditcards, or other financial assets, making it impossible for them to make independent financial decisions.

3. Financial Manipulation and Coercion:

The abuser may manipulate or coerce the victim into making financial decisions that benefit them, even if it's at the victim's expense. This could include forcing the victim to take out loans, co-sign on debt, or invest in risky ventures without their full understanding or consent.

4. Financial Isolation:

The abuser may try to isolate the victim from their family, friends, and support systems, making it difficult for them to seek help or advice. This could involve preventing the victim from having access to a phone or internet, or limiting their contact with loved ones who might offer support.

5. Making All Financial Decisions:

The abuser may insist on making all financial decisions, leaving the victim with no say in how their own money is managed. This could involve controlling the victim's spending, forcing them to make financial decisions that they are uncomfortable with, or preventing them from seeking financial advice from others.

6. Using Financial Control as a Weapon:

The abuser may use financial control as a form of punishment or control, withholding money or resources as away to exert power and influence the victim's behavior. This could involve refusing to pay for essential expenses, limiting the victim's access to food or transportation, or threatening to cut off their financial support altogether.

7. Gaslighting and Denial:

The abuser may gaslight the victim into believing that they are financially incompetent or that their concerns about financial abuse are unfounded. They may deny that they are controlling the victim's finances, minimizing the impact of their behavior, or blaming the victim for their own financial problems.

8. Financial Sabotage:

The abuser may sabotage the victim's financial stability by intentionally damaging their credit score, running up their debts, or taking actions that jeopardize their financial security. This could involve ruining the victim's credit history, opening credit cards in their name without their knowledge, or making financial decisions that put their future at risk.

9. Withholding Information about Finances:

The abuser may withhold vital financial information from the victim, such as the amount of income they earn, their financial liabilities, or any changes in their financial situation. This lack of transparency makes it impossible for the victim to make informed financial decisions and increases their vulnerability to manipulation and abuse.

10. Making the Victim Feel Dependent:

The abuser may make the victim feel financially dependent on them, reinforcing the idea that they cannot survive without their financial support. This could involve making the victim responsible for all household expenses, while they control the purse strings, creating a power imbalance that leaves the victim vulnerable to abuse.

11. Using Threats and Intimidation:

The abuser may threaten to cut off the victim's financial support, or threaten to take away their children or belongings if they don't comply with their demands. This fear-mongering tactic is designed to keep the victim under control and prevents them from seeking help or attempting to leave the abusive relationship.

12. Controlling the Victim's Employment:

The abuser may control the victim's employment, forcing them to quit their job, take on a less desirable position, or preventing them from working altogether. This can leave the victim financially dependent on the abuser and further isolate them from their support systems.

13. Manipulating the Victim's Debt:

The abuser may manipulate the victim's debt, forcing them to take on loans or credit card debt without their full understanding or consent. This could involve hiding the extent of their debt from the victim or making them responsible for debt that they did not incur.

14. Controlling the Victim's Property:

The abuser may control the victim's property, preventing them from accessing or selling their belongings without their permission. This could involve taking control of the victim's car, house, or other assets, leaving them with little to no financial security.

15. Using Financial Abuse to Control the Victim's Life:

The abuser may use financial abuse to control the victim's entire life, preventing them from making any decisions without their consent. This could involve controlling the victim's access to education, healthcare, or even their ability to move freely.

Recognizing these signs of financial abuse is crucial for victims to understand the nature of their situation and to seek help. It's important to remember that financial abuse is not a one-time incident; it's a pattern of behavior that is designed to control and manipulate the victim.

Beyond the Signs: Recognizing the Patterns

While these signs are helpful indicators, it's essential to recognize that financial abuse often operates within a broader pattern of controlling and coercive behavior. It may be accompanied by other forms of abuse, such as physical, emotional, or sexual abuse.

Financial abuse can be subtle and insidious, often disguised as "helping" or "managing" finances. It may not always be obvious at first, and victims may be hesitant to admit that they are experiencing abuse. They may be embarrassed, ashamed, or afraid of losing the abuser's support.

Breaking Free from the Cycle

Financial abuse can have a devastating impact on victims' lives, leaving them feeling trapped, isolated, and powerless. It can erode their self- esteem, undermine their confidence, and prevent them from achieving their full potential.

However, it is important to remember that you are not alone. There are resources and support systems available to help you break free from the cycle of financial abuse.

Here are some steps you can take to start reclaiming your financial independence and safety:

Seek Professional Help:

A therapist, counselor, or social worker can provide support, guidance, and a safe space to discuss your experiences. They can help you develop a plan to escape the abuse and rebuild your life.

Connect with Support Groups:

Sharing your story with others who have experiencedfinancial abuse can provide invaluable validation and support. Support groups can offer a sense of community and belonging, and they can help you understand that you are not alone.

Develop a Financial Safety Plan:

A financial safety plan can help you regain control of your finances, build financial security, and protect yourself from future abuse. This plan may include steps such as opening a separate bank account, obtaining credit cards in your own name, and budgeting your expenses.

Seek Legal Assistance:

A lawyer can help you understand your legal rights, explore your options for divorce or separation, and protect your financial assets from the abuser.

Build a Network of Support:

Reach out to trusted friends, family members, or community organizations for support and guidance. They can provide emotional support, practical assistance, and a safe space for you to process your experiences.

Remembering Your Strength:

Financial abuse is a form of control, but it doesn't have to define your life. You are not weak or incompetent. You are strong, resilient, and deserving of a life free from abuse.

Breaking free from financial abuse may be a challenging journey, but it is a journey worth taking. You have the power to reclaim your financial independence, rebuild your life, and create a brighter future for yourself.

Remember that you are not alone, and there is help available.

Remember: Financial abuse is a form of domestic violence, and you deserve to be treated with respect, dignity, and safety. If you are experiencing financial abuse, know that you are not alone and there are people who care and want to help.

CHAPTER THREE

Tactics Of Control And Manipulation

Financial abuse is a subtle and insidious form of control that can leave victims feeling trapped and powerless. Abusers often use a variety of tactics to exert financial control, isolating their victims, manipulating their finances, and ultimately stripping them of their independence. This section will delve into the various methods abusers employ to establish and maintain their financial dominance, revealing the intricate web of control they weave.

The Power of Control:

The abuser's goal is to establish complete financial control over their victim, often through a calculated process of manipulation and coercion. This control extends beyond access to money and resources, encompassing decision-making power, information, and the victim's overall financial well-being. The tactics employed are not always overt or obvious, often disguised as acts of love or concern, making it even harder for victims to recognize the true nature of the abuse.

1. Isolating the Victim:

One of the first steps an abuser takes is to isolate their victim from their support system, cutting them off from friends, family, and anyone who might provide a different perspective or offer help. This isolation is crucial to the abuser's plan, as it limits the victim's access to information, resources, and potential allies. It creates a sense of dependency and fosters the belief that the abuser is the only source of support and guidance.

Restricting Access to Communication:

Abusers may monitor phone calls, text messages, and email accounts, limiting the victim's ability to communicate with others. They might even confiscate phones or restrict access to the internet.

Controlling Social Interactions:

They might discourage the victim from socializing with friends or family, making excuses for their absence, or even physically preventing them from attending social gatherings.

Undermining Relationships:

Abusers may spread rumors about the victim's friends or family, sowing seeds of doubt and distrust, making it harder for the victim to rely on their support network.

2. Controlling Finances and Resources:

Once the victim is isolated, the abuser starts tightening their grip on finances, gradually assuming control over all aspects of their financial life. This control can take various forms, each designed to weaken the victim's financial independence and limit their ability to make decisions about their own money.

Controlling Access to Money:

The abuser might insist on managing all the finances, denying the victim access to shared accounts or even their own personal income. This could involve controlling the flow of money for everyday expenses, refusing to share financial information, or forcing the victim to request funds for even basic needs.

Financial Invisibility:

The abuser may keep the victim in the dark about finances, refusing to discuss the household budget, investment decisions, or even the family's overall financial standing. This lack of information makes it impossible for the victim to make informed financial decisions and further strengthens their dependence on the abuser.

Preventing Financial Independence:

Abusers may discourage their victims from pursuing education or employment opportunities, limiting their access to job training or financial resources that could enhance their earning potential. This keeps the victim financially dependent and reliant on the abuser's control.

3. Manipulation and Deception:

Abusers often rely on manipulative tactics to control their victims' finances, exploiting their emotional vulnerabilities and creating a sense of guilt, obligation, or fear. These tactics are often subtle, weaving a web of financial control disguised as caring or concern.

Guilt and Obligation:

The abuser may use guilt and obligation to manipulate the victim into making financial decisions that benefit them. They might make promises of financial security or future rewards to incentivize the victim to give up control of their finances.

Financial Threats:

The abuser might threaten to withhold financial support or resources if the victim does not comply with their demands. This instills fear and anxiety in the victim, making them feel trapped and desperate to appease the abuser.

Financial Lies and Deception:

Abusers may lie about their financial situation, debts, or spending habits, creating a false sense of security or keeping the victim in the dark about their true financial standing.

4. Emotional Manipulation:

The emotional toll of financial abuse is significant, often leaving victims feeling powerless, trapped, and isolated. The abuser's manipulation tactics create a sense of dependence and make it difficult for victims to recognize the abuse or seek help.

Shame and Self-Blame:

Abusers often use language that makes victims feel ashamed of their financial situation or decisions. They might belittle the victim's financial abilities, casting doubt on their judgment and making them feel unworthy of financial independence.

Fear of Abandonment:

Abusers may threaten to leave the relationship if the victim does not comply with their financial demands. This creates a fear of abandonment, making the victim desperate to maintain the relationship, even at the cost of their financial independence.

Love and Loyalty:

Abusers may use expressions of love and loyalty to manipulate the victim into relinquishing financial control. They might portray themselves as the provider and protector, suggesting that the victim is incapable of managing finances on their own.

5. Eroding Trust and Independence:

Over time, these tactics chip away at the victim's self-confidence and erode their sense of autonomy. They begin to question their own abilities, rely on the abuser for financial guidance, and lose faith in their ability to make sound financial decisions.

Breaking the Cycle:

Recognizing the tactics of financial abuse is the first step towards breaking free. Understanding the underlying mechanisms of control and manipulation allows victims to see through the abuser's facade and start reclaiming their financial independence.

Moving Forward:

Seek Professional Help:

Reach out to a trusted friend, family member, or a domestic violence advocate for support and guidance.

Build a Support System:

Connect with friends, family, or support groups who understand the complexities of financial abuse.

Educate Yourself:

Learn about financial literacy, budgeting, and managing your finances independently.

Develop a Safety Plan:

Create a plan for financial independence, including steps for securing housing, resources, and financial support.

Empower Yourself:

Remember that you are not alone, and there is help available. Take steps to regain your financial independence and break free from the cycle of abuse.

The journey to financial independence may be challenging, but it is possible. By understanding the tactics of financial abuse, seeking support, and taking control of your finances, you can reclaim your power and create a secure future for yourself.

CHAPTER FOUR

The Emotional And Psychological Impact

⚜

Financial abuse, a cruel form of control, casts a long shadow over the lives of its victims, leaving them emotionally and psychologically scarred. The invisible chains of financial manipulation bind them, eroding their sense of self-worth and hindering their ability to move forward. The emotional toll of financial abuse is profound, a silent torment that can linger long after the abuser is gone.

Imagine a life where your every financial decision is scrutinized, where you are constantly denied access to your own money, and where you are forced to justify every expenditure. This is the reality for many victims of financial abuse. The constant feeling of being trapped, controlled, and financially dependent on an abuser can be deeply demoralizing, fostering a sense of helplessness and hopelessness.

The emotional consequences of financial abuse are often intertwined with other forms of domestic violence, creating a complex web of trauma.

Victims may experience a range of emotions, including:

Fear and Anxiety:

The constant fear of financial instability, the potential for losing everything, and the threat of further abuse can create a pervasive sense of anxiety. Victims often live in a state of high alert, anticipating the next act of financial control.

Shame and Guilt:

Abusers often skillfully manipulate their victims, making them feel responsible for the financial hardships they experience. This can lead to intense feelings of shame and guilt, further isolating them and preventing them from reaching out for help.

Depression and Low Self-Esteem:

Financial abuse undermines a victim's sense of self-worth and independence. They may begin to question their own abilities and judgment, believing they are not capable of managing their finances effectively. This can lead to depression, anxiety, and a loss of motivation.

Anger and Resentment:

The feeling of being robbed of financial control and autonomy can fuel anger and resentment towards the abuser. Victims may struggle to reconcile their feelings of love and loyalty with the abuse they are enduring.

Isolation and Dependency:

Financial abuse often goes hand in hand with isolation. Abusers may limit their victims' access to friends, family, and outside resources, increasing their dependency on the abuser for financial support. This isolation makes it harder for victims to recognize and seek help for the abuse they are experiencing.

The emotional impact of financial abuse can have lasting consequences, extending far beyond the immediate

relationship. Victims may struggle to rebuild their lives, facing challenges in managing their finances independently, establishing financial stability, and trusting future partners. They may also develop unhealthy financial habits, such as avoidance and fear of making financial decisions.

Beyond the emotional toll, financial abuse can also have significant psychological effects on victims:

Cognitive Dissonance:

Financial abuse can create a cognitive dissonance within victims, leading to internal conflict and confusion. They may struggle to reconcile their own values and beliefs with the abusive behavior they are experiencing, questioning their own sanity and judgment.

Trauma Bonding:

Abusers often employ a cycle of abuse, alternating periods of kindness and affection with periods of control and manipulation. This can create a sense of dependence and attachment, making it difficult for victims to leave, even whenthey recognize the abuse.

Post-Traumatic Stress Disorder (PTSD):

The constant fear, anxiety, and emotional distress associated with financial abuse can trigger PTSD symptoms in some victims. This can manifest in flashbacks, nightmares, and hypervigilance, interfering with their daily lives.

Dissociation:

As a coping mechanism, some victims may dissociate, emotionally detaching themselves from their experiences. This can be a way of protecting themselves from the overwhelming pain and emotional turmoil caused by financial abuse.

Understanding the psychological and emotional consequences of financial abuse is crucial for supporting victims in their journey to recovery. It is essential to validate their experiences, acknowledge the trauma they have endured, and empower them to take back control of their lives.

Recognizing the signs of financial abuse, understanding the dynamics of power imbalance, and developing strategies for regaining financial independence are all essential steps in breaking the cycle of abuse.

However, it is equally important to address the emotional and psychological wounds inflicted by financial control.

Providing Support and Healing:

Supporting victims of financial abuse requires a multi-faceted approach that addresses both the practical and emotional aspects of their recovery. Here are some ways to provide support and promote healing:

Empathy and Validation:

Listen attentively to victims without judgment or criticism. Acknowledge the emotional pain they are experiencing and validate their feelings. Let them know that they are not alone and that their experiences are valid.

Educating and Empowering:

Provide information about financial abuse, its impact, and resources available for support. Help victims understand that they are not responsible for the abuser's actions and that they have the right to financial independence.

Creating Safety Plans:

Collaborate with victims to develop a comprehensive safety plan that addresses their financial needs. This may include seeking legal advice, exploring options for housing, and developing a budget for financial stability.

Connecting with Support Services:

Refer victims to domestic violence shelters, legal aid organizations, financial counseling services, and mental health professionals who can provide specialized support.

Building a Support Network:

Encourage victims to connect with trusted friends, family members, or support groups who can offer emotional support and practical assistance.

Therapy and Counseling:

Therapy can be invaluable in processing trauma, rebuilding self-esteem, and learning coping mechanisms. Therapists can provide a safe space for victims to explore their emotions, develop healthy coping strategies, and address the psychological impact of financial abuse.

Breaking the Silence:

It is vital to break the silence surrounding financial abuse. By sharing personal stories, raising awareness, and challenging societal norms, we can create a more supportive environment for victims and empower them to seek help.

Financial abuse is a form of domestic violence, and it is never acceptable. By working together, we can ensure that victims have the resources and support they need to reclaim their financial freedom and build a life free from abuse.

The road to recovery from financial abuse is long and challenging, but it is not insurmountable. With the right support, victims can heal from the emotional and psychological wounds inflicted by their abuser, rebuild their financial lives, and find hope for a brighter future.

Remember, you are not alone. There are resources and support systems available to help you break free from the cycle of financial abuse and reclaim your financial independence and well-being.

CHAPTER FIVE
Sharing Stories

The stories of survivors are the heart of this book. They are the voices that break the silence, exposing the hidden truth of financial abuse and giving hope to others who are struggling. Each individual's journey is unique, reflecting the diverse ways financial control can manifest in relationships.

Let's begin with Sarah, a young woman whose story illustrates the insidious nature of financial abuse. As a newlywed, Sarah's husband, David, gradually assumed control of their finances. He insisted on managing their joint account, claiming he was better with money. He discouraged her from having her own bank account, telling her it was unnecessary and would complicate things. Sarah, trusting and wanting to support her husband, complied.

Over time, Sarah found herself increasingly isolated. David restricted her access to money, dictating what she could buy and how much she could spend. He would accuse her of being frivolous or irresponsible, blaming her for their financial woes. Sarah began to feel trapped and powerless, her self-esteem eroded as David's control tightened. He used their shared finances as a tool for manipulation, withholding money as punishment for his perceived transgressions.

Sarah's story resonates with countless others. They were often lured into relationships with promises of security and stability, only to find their financial independence gradually chipped away. Like Sarah, they learned to live with the constant fear of being caught, the dread of being accused of being irresponsible or ungrateful. They carried the burden of their abusers' financial decisions, constantly striving to please, to prove their worth, and to avoid further restrictions.

Another survivor, Michael, tells a story that sheds light on the complexities of financial abuse within same-sex relationships. Michael was in a long- term partnership with his partner, Mark. As the relationship progressed, Mark started taking more control over their joint finances, using Michael's income for his own expenses while limiting Michael's access to funds.

Mark justified this by claiming he was the "breadwinner" and Michael should be grateful for his generosity.

This scenario highlights the crucial point that financial abuse transcends gender and can occur in any relationship dynamic. The power imbalance is often what dictates the abuser's behavior, regardless of sexual orientation or gender identity. Michael's experience exposes the need to address the issue within diverse communities, breaking down the misconceptions that financial abuse is solely a "female" issue.

These stories are not merely anecdotal; they are powerful testaments to the devastating impact of financial abuse. They expose the tactics abusers use to isolate and control their victims, dismantling their sense of autonomy and self-worth. They demonstrate the psychological and emotional damage inflicted by financial control, leaving victims feeling trapped and powerless.

However, the stories also illustrate resilience and hope. Sarah, after enduring years of abuse, eventually found the strength to leave David. She sought legal aid, obtained a restraining order, and began rebuilding her life. Michael, too, found the courage to challenge his partner's financial control.He sought professional guidance and worked towards financial independence, eventually severing the toxic relationship.

The resilience of these survivors inspires others who are currently facing financial abuse. Their journeys offer a beacon of hope, proving that escape is possible. They demonstrate that with support, knowledge, and determination, individuals can reclaim their financial freedom and build a secure future.

It is essential to acknowledge that each survivor's story is unique, reflecting the diverse ways financial abuse can manifest in relationships. The stories highlight the need for a nuanced understanding of financial abuse, moving beyond the stereotypes that often limit the perception of this complex issue.

Here are some key takeaways from these survivor stories:

Financial abuse is not always overt.

It can be subtle and manipulative, making it difficult to recognize and even harder to identify as abuse.

Financial abuse often goes hand-in-hand with other forms of domestic violence.

It is a means to control and isolate victims, making them dependent on their abuser.

The consequences of financial abuse can be long-lasting.

Victims may experience financial instability, credit damage, and emotional trauma long after escaping the relationship.

There is hope for recovery.

With support and guidance, victims can reclaim their financial independence and rebuild their lives.

The narratives of survivors are crucial in raising awareness about financial abuse. By sharing their stories, they empower others to recognize the signs, seek help, and break free from the cycle of abuse. Their resilience and determination offer a powerful message of hope, demonstrating that financial independence is achievable even after enduring the trauma of financial abuse.

These are just a few examples of the many stories that paint a stark picture of financial abuse. By amplifying these voices, we can shed light on this hidden form of domestic violence and work towards a future where everyone has the right to financial security and autonomy.

CHAPTER SIX

Understanding Power Imbalance

Financial abuse thrives on a power imbalance, a dynamic where one partner wields disproportionate control over the finances and resources within the relationship. This power imbalance is not merely about money; it's a manifestation of control, manipulation, and a desire to maintain dominance. Abusers often use financial means to isolate, intimidate, and restrict their victims, creating a web of dependence and fear.

Imagine Sarah, a young woman starting her career, meeting a charming man, Mark. He showered her with affection and extravagant gifts, making her feel cherished and loved. However, as their relationship progressed, subtle shifts began to occur. Mark started handling all their finances, claiming he was "better with money." Sarah, initially trusting and happy, allowed him to manage their joint accounts. Soon, she realized she needed his permission for even the smallest purchases. Mark would dismiss her concerns, saying, "Don't worry, I'll take care of everything." Over time, Sarah felt increasingly isolated and financially dependent on Mark. She lost her sense of financial independence, her self-esteem eroded, and her ability to make her own decisions dwindled. This, in essence, is the hallmark of financial abuse.

The power imbalance in financial abuse can be rooted in various factors:

1. Financial Dependence:

When one partner is financially dependent on the other, the abuser gains significant leverage. The victim might rely on the abuser for income, housing, or basic needs. The abuser can exploit this dependence, threatening to withhold resources or even evict the victim if they challenge the abuser's control.

2. Economic Insecurity:

Abusers often prey on individuals struggling with financial insecurity. This could be due to unemployment, low income, or past financial mismanagement. Abusers may exploit their victims' vulnerability by offering false promises of financial security, only to manipulate and exploit them once they become dependent.

3. Lack of Financial Knowledge:

Limited financial literacy can make individuals more susceptible to financial abuse. Abusers may exploit their victims' lack of understanding about finances, making them feel incapable of managing their money. The abuser might use complex financial terminology, shroud transactions in secrecy, or even use fake financial documents to create a sense of confusion and dependence.

4. Social Isolation:

Abusers frequently isolate their victims, limiting their access to family, friends, or external support systems. This isolation prevents victims from seeking help, sharing their experiences, or gaining independent advice. Without a support network, victims become more vulnerable to the abuser's control and manipulation.

5. Control over Resources:

The abuser often controls the access to shared resources. They may have sole access to bank accounts, credit cards, or even restrict the victim's ability to earn income. By controlling the financial resources, the abuser can limit the victim's autonomy and make them dependent on the abuser's goodwill.

6. Psychological Manipulation:

The abuser uses psychological manipulation tactics to reinforce the power imbalance. They might use guilt, shame, or fear to control the victim's behavior. For example, an abuser might accuse the victim of being "irresponsible" with money or threaten to leave if they don't comply with the abuser's financial demands.

7. Legal Barriers:

Victims of financial abuse often face legal barriers that hinder their ability to escape the abuse. These barriers can include:

Lack of awareness:

Many victims don't recognize the signs of financial abuse, making it challenging to seek legal protection.

Complex legal processes:

The legal system can be overwhelming, and victims might feel intimidated by the process of obtaining legal aid, filing restraining orders, or seeking financial restitution.

Limited resources:

Many victims lack access to legal representation, making it difficult to fight for their rights in court.

Lack of support:

Victims might face disbelief or judgment from friends, family, or even legal professionals, making it harder to gain the support they need to leave the abusive relationship.

The power imbalance in financial abuse creates a vicious cycle. The abuser maintains control over the finances, leading to the victim's dependence and isolation. The victim, lacking financial independence and support, finds it increasingly difficult to break free. This cycle often escalates, leading to further manipulation, coercion, and exploitation.

It's essential to remember that financial abuse is not always about outright theft or extravagant spending. It's about control, manipulation, and undermining the victim's ability to make their own financial decisions.

Even subtle acts of control, such as making the victim feel guilty about spending money, can be a form of financial abuse.

Recognizing the power dynamics at play in financial abuse is crucial for both victims and those who support them. Understanding these dynamics can help break the cycle of abuse and empower individuals to reclaim their financial freedom and rebuild their lives.

CHAPTER SEVEN

A Vicious Cycle

The insidious nature of financial abuse often lies in its ability to isolate victims, making them increasingly dependent on their abuser. This isolation is not merely physical; it extends to emotional, social, and financial spheres, creating a web of control that is difficult to break free from. Abusers understand the power of isolation, using it as a tool to chip away at their victim's sense of self-worth and autonomy. They manipulate circumstances to limit the victim's access to resources, support networks, and even basic information, leaving them feeling trapped and powerless.

One of the primary ways abusers achieve isolation is by limiting their victim's contact with friends and family. They may discourage or outright prohibit visits, phone calls, or even communication through social media. This isolation serves multiple purposes. Firstly, it deprives the victim of a vital support system, making it harder to confide in someone about the abuse they are experiencing. Without an outside perspective, the victim may begin to question their own reality and doubt their perceptions of the abuser's actions. Secondly, isolation allows the abuser to exert greater control over the victim's narrative. By controlling the information that the victim receives and the people they interact with, the abuser can paint a distorted picture of their relationship, minimizing or even denying the abuse.

Financial abuse often goes hand-in-hand with emotional and physical manipulation. Abusers may use financial control to isolate their victims further, limiting their access to money and resources. This can take various forms, such as controlling access to bank accounts, withholding funds, or forcing the victim to depend entirely on the abuser for financial support. As the victim becomes increasingly reliant on the abuser for financial survival, they may feel unable to leave the relationship, fearing they will be left destitute and without means. This fear of financial insecurity can be a powerful tool for manipulation, keeping the victim trapped in the abusive cycle.

Beyond limiting access to finances, abusers may employ tactics to control their victim's employment or career aspirations. They may discourage their partner from pursuing education or professional opportunities, limiting their earning potential and further entrenching their dependency. This tactic not only diminishes the victim's financial independence but also undermines their sense of self-worth and agency. The abuser may use belittling comments or threats to discourage the victim from pursuing career goals, making them feel incompetent or incapable of achieving success.

Isolation often involves a gradual process of erosion, chipping away at the victim's sense of self and autonomy. As the abuser's control tightens, the victim may begin to withdraw from social activities, neglecting their personal interests and hobbies. They may feel drained and exhausted, both emotionally and physically, due to the constant stress and anxiety of living in a controlling environment. This withdrawal from social connections can lead to feelings of loneliness, isolation, and depression.

Another tactic abusers use to foster dependency is by minimizing or denying the victim's skills and abilities. They may belittle their partner's accomplishments, dismissing their opinions, and questioning their judgment. This constant undermining of the victim's confidence makes them more susceptible to manipulation and control. The abuser may create a false sense of incompetence, making the victim feel unable to manage their own finances or make independent decisions. This can lead to a cycle of dependency, where the victim relies on the abuser for guidance and decision-making in all aspects of their lives.

Isolation also extends to limiting the victim's access to information. Abusers may control the victim's access to the internet, phone calls, or even news sources. This can leave the victim feeling isolated and uninformed, further decreasing their ability to make informed decisions and seek help. The lack of information can also make it difficult for the victim to understand the extent of the abuse they are experiencing and recognize the signs of financial control.

The manipulation and control tactics employed by abusers can have a profound impact on the victim's mental and emotional well-being. They may experience feelings of anxiety, depression, low self-esteem, and hopelessness. This can lead to a decline in physical health, as constant stress and lack of control take a toll on the body. Victims may also experience difficulties in their relationships with family and friends, as they struggle to navigate the complex dynamics of their abusive relationship.

To break free from the vicious cycle of isolation and dependency, it's crucial to understand the tactics abusers use and their impact on the victim's mental and emotional well-being. Recognizing these tactics is the first step towards reclaiming autonomy and achieving financial independence. Victims need to understand that they are not alone and that there are resources available to help them escape the abusive relationship and rebuild their lives.

It is important to note that the dynamics of financial abuse are complex and multifaceted. The tactics employed by abusers can vary depending on the individual, the relationship, and the circumstances. However, understanding the underlying principles of isolation and dependency is essential for identifying and addressing financial abuse in all its forms.

This section has explored how abusers use isolation tactics to increase dependency and maintain control. Isolation is a core element in financial abuse, as it creates a power imbalance that allows the abuser to manipulate and control the victim's finances and overall well-being. By understanding the ways in which abusers manipulate isolation, victims can begin to identify the signs of financial abuse and take steps towards reclaiming their financial autonomy and independence.

CHAPTER EIGHT

From Guilt To Fear

The insidious nature of financial abuse lies not just in the tangible deprivation but also in the psychological manipulation that underpins it. Abusers often employ a range of tactics, designed to erode their victims' sense of self-worth, independence, and even sanity. These manipulations can be subtle, insidious, and often difficult to recognize, making them even more damaging. One of the most common tactics is

guilt tripping

The abuser might make their victim feel responsible for their financial struggles, suggesting they are not working hard enough, spending too much, or not managing money properly. This can lead to feelings of inadequacy and self-blame, making the victim more likely to accept the abuser's control over finances. A classic example is the abuser blaming the victim for not earning enough money, saying things like, "If you only worked harder, we wouldn't be struggling." This tactic subtly shifts the responsibility for financial hardship onto the victim, making them feel like they are failing and need to appease the abuser.

Another common technique is

fear mongering

The abuser might threaten to leave, take the children, or cut off financial support if the victim doesn't comply with their demands.

This fear can be paralyzing, forcing the victim to submit to the abuser's control for the sake of their own survival and the well-being of their family. The abuser might say, "If you keep spending money like this, I'm going to leave you and take the kids." This type of threat creates a constant sense of fear and insecurity, making it harder for the victim to assert their own needs and desires.

Gaslighting

is another insidious manipulation tactic often employed by financial abusers. This is a form of psychological manipulation where the abuser denies reality or distorts facts to make the victim question their own sanity. This might involve denying spending money, claiming the victim is misremembering financial transactions, or making them doubt their own financial abilities. For example, the abuser might say, "You're crazy, I never said that," or "You're always making things up." This tactic undermines the victim's self-confidence and makes them less likely to challenge the abuser's financial control.

Isolation

is another powerful tool used by financial abusers to increase dependency and maintain control. The abuser might discourage the victim from spending time with friends or family, claiming they are bad influences or are trying to manipulate the victim. They might even control the victim's access to social media or communication devices, further isolating them. This isolation makes it harder for the victim to seek support or advice from others, increasing their reliance on the abuser and making them more vulnerable to manipulation.

Love bombing

is a tactic often used in the early stages of the relationship, characterized by excessive attention, affection, and gifts. This tactic can create a sense of dependence and obligation, making the victim feel grateful and indebted to the abuser. The abuser might shower the victim with lavish gifts and promises of a wonderful future, making them believe they have found their soulmate. However, this love bombing is usually a facade used to manipulate the victim into accepting the abuser's control.

Financial abusers may also engage in :

emotional manipulation, playing on their victim's emotions to gain control over their finances. They might use tears, anger, or guilt to make the victim feel responsible for their emotional well-being. The abuser might say, "You're making me so sad," or "You're the reason I'm so stressed out." This manipulation makes the victim feel obligated to meet the abuser's needs, even at the expense of their own financial security.

Financial abusers often use ***denial and rationalization***

to justify their controlling behavior. They might downplay their actions, claiming they are simply "helping" or "protecting" their partner. They might also blame the victim for their financial situation, saying they are "irresponsible" or "spendthrift." This denial and rationalization can make it difficult for the victim to recognize the abuse and seek help.

Playing the victim

is another manipulative tactic where the abuser portrays themselves as the victim of the situation, deflecting responsibility for their own actions. They might blame the victim for their financial problems, claiming they are being mistreated or that the victim is trying to control them. This tactic can be particularly effective in confusing the victim and making them question their own perception of the situation.

Threats and intimidation

are often used by financial abusers to enforce their control. This might involve threats of physical violence, threats of leaving, or threats of taking away the children. The abuser might also use intimidation tactics, such as yelling, slamming doors, or making threatening gestures. These tactics create an atmosphere of fear and coercion, making the victim afraid to challenge the abuser's financial control.

Financial abuse is a complex and insidious form of domestic violence

, often operating under the radar. The psychological manipulations employed by abusers are designed to break down their victims' self-esteem, independence, and sense of reality, leaving them feeling trapped and powerless. Recognizing these tactics and understanding the psychological dynamics at play is crucial for breaking the cycle of abuse and reclaiming financial freedom.

CHAPTER NINE

The Role Of Gender In Financial Abuse

The intricate interplay between gender and financial abuse unveils a complex dynamic rooted in societal expectations and deeply ingrained gender roles. While financial abuse can affect individuals regardless of gender, it is crucial to recognize the unique ways in which gender norms exacerbate this form of violence against women.

Traditional gender roles often place women in positions of economic vulnerability, making them more susceptible to financial abuse.

Historically, women have been expected to prioritize domestic responsibilities, leading to limited access to education, employment opportunities, and financial independence. This societal conditioning can create a power imbalance within relationships, leaving women financially dependent on their partners and more susceptible to manipulation and control.

One prominent example is the "breadwinner" stereotype, which perpetuates the notion that men are primarily responsible for providing financial support, while women focus on household chores and childcare. This expectation can create a dynamic where women are less likely to manage family finances or have independent income streams. This dependence on their partners can make it difficult for women to recognize or escape financial abuse, as they may feel they lack the resources to support themselves or their children independently. Furthermore, the societal devaluation of traditionally "feminine" professions can contribute to financial vulnerability. While women have made significant strides in the workforce, gender wage gaps persist across various industries, limiting women's earning potential and increasing their reliance on male partners for financial stability. This disparity can create a sense of financial inferiority, making women more susceptible to abusers' manipulation and control over finances.

In addition to economic disparities, societal expectations about women's roles in relationships can also contribute to financial abuse. The notion that women should be "submissive," "supportive," and "dependent" on their partners can normalize financial control and manipulation. Abusers exploit these societal expectations, employing guilt, fear, and emotional manipulation to restrict their partners' access to money, forcing them to rely on the abuser for basic needs.

For instance, abusers may control access to shared bank accounts, limit spending on personal necessities, or withhold funds for education or professional development. This financial control can be used to isolate women, preventing them from pursuing their personal goals or escaping abusive relationships.

The cycle of financial abuse is often intertwined with other forms of domestic violence, creating a complex web of control and coercion. Abusers may use financial abuse to punish their partners, instill fear, and maintain power within the relationship. For example, withholding money for groceries or childcare can create a constant sense of anxiety and dependence, making it challenging for victims to leave the abusive situation.

Moreover, financial abuse can have long-term consequences for women, affecting their financial independence, career development, and overall well-being. This can lead to increased reliance on social services, limited access to education, and difficulty in achieving financial stability.

Understanding the intersection of gender and financial abuse is critical for effectively addressing this issue. By challenging societal expectations and promoting gender equality, we can empower women to achieve financial independence and break free from abusive relationships. Recognizing the unique vulnerabilities faced by women in financially abusive situations allows us to create support systems and resources tailored to their needs.

Financial abuse is a serious issue with far-reaching consequences for victims, and understanding the role of gender in its perpetuation is crucial for finding effective solutions. By acknowledging the power imbalances, societal pressures, and economic disparities that contribute to financial abuse against women, we can create a safer and more equitable environment for all individuals.

Moving forward, it is essential to continue challenging gender stereotypes and promoting financial literacy for both women and men. Empowering women to develop financial independence and access to resources is a vital step in breaking the cycle of financial abuse. Providing education, counseling, and support services tailored to women's specific needs can play a crucial role in their recovery and empowerment.

Ultimately, addressing financial abuse requires a multifaceted approach that addresses both individual experiences and societal structures. By working together, we can create a society where financial abuse is recognized, understood, and effectively prevented.

CHAPTER TEN

Legal And Societal Challenges Faced By Victims

The legal and societal landscape can be a labyrinth of obstacles for victims of financial abuse, often hindering their ability to seek help and escape the cycle of control. The very systems designed to protect can become entangled in complexities, leaving victims feeling isolated and powerless.

One of the most significant legal hurdles is the challenge of proving financial abuse. Unlike physical violence, financial control often leaves no visible scars. Gathering evidence can be a daunting task, requiring meticulous documentation of every transaction, every instance of coercion, and every veiled threat. Victims may be hesitant to involve law enforcement, fearing retaliation from their abuser or a lack of understanding from authorities who may view financial abuse as a mere "money problem."

Moreover, legal definitions of financial abuse can be ambiguous and vary widely across jurisdictions. In some areas, financial abuse may not be recognized as a distinct crime, leading to limited legal remedies and support. Victims may find themselves facing legal battles that require extensive resources and legal expertise, further exacerbating their financial vulnerability.

Beyond the legal realm, societal perceptions and cultural norms can further compound the challenges faced by victims. Financial abuse is often seen as a private matter, a "family issue" to be dealt with within the household.

This perception can lead to a lack of public awareness and a reluctance to intervene. Victims may encounter disbelief or judgment from loved ones, friends, or even professional advisors who may not fully grasp the gravity of the situation. Furthermore, societal pressures around gender roles and financial dependence can play a significant role in perpetuating financial abuse. Women, historically expected to be financially reliant on their partners, may face additional obstacles in seeking independence. They may be discouraged from pursuing education or employment opportunities, leaving them trapped in a cycle of financial dependency and control. This dynamic applies to men as well, as societal expectations around masculinity can prevent them from seeking help or disclosing instances of financial abuse, leading to feelings of shame and isolation.

The economic realities of escaping an abusive relationship further complicate the situation. Victims often face a daunting task of rebuilding their financial lives from scratch. They may have limited access to savings, credit, or even a stable income. The fear of financial instability and the perceived burden of becoming financially independent can act as powerful deterrents, keeping victims trapped in abusive relationships.

The societal and legal challenges faced by victims of financial abuse are multifaceted and interconnected. They stem from a lack of awareness, understanding, and adequate support systems. Addressing these challenges requires a shift in societal attitudes, improved legal frameworks, and increased access to resources and support networks. Victims need to know that they are not alone, that their experiences are valid, and that help is available. By fostering a culture of awareness, empathy, and support, we can break down the barriers that hinder victims from seeking help and achieving financial freedom.

CHAPTER ELEVEN

Breaking The Cycle: Strategies For Empowerment

While the legal and societal hurdles can be daunting, it is vital to remember that victims of financial abuse are not powerless. There are steps they can take to reclaim their financial independence and break free from the cycle of control.

1. Seek Information and Support:

The first step is to educate yourself about financial abuse. Learn the tactics abusers use, understand your rights, and seek out resources that can provide support and guidance. Organizations dedicated to domestic violence, financial literacy, and legal aid can provide valuable information and resources.

2. Document and Secure Evidence:

Maintaining detailed records of financial transactions, communication logs, and instances of manipulation is crucial. This documentation can serve as evidence in legal proceedings and aid in building a case against the abuser.

3. Develop a Financial Safety Plan:

Create a plan to secure your financial future, including steps to access credit, establish bank accounts, and build a support network.

Consider opening a separate bank account that your abuser does not have access to, and take steps to manage your debt responsibly.

4. Seek Legal Counsel:

Legal professionals can help navigate the complex legal landscape and advocate for your rights. They can provide guidance on obtaining restraining orders, protecting assets, and pursuing legal remedies for financial abuse.

5. Build a Support Network:

Seek support from trusted friends, family members, therapists, or support groups. Having a strong network of people who understand your situation can provide emotional support, practical advice, and a sense of community.

6. Prioritize Self-Care:

Financial abuse can take a significant toll on mental and emotional well- being. Make time for self-care activities, such as exercise, relaxation techniques, and spending time with loved ones. Prioritizing your well- being is essential in overcoming the psychological effects of abuse.

7. Educate Others:

Sharing your story and raising awareness about financial abuse can help break down the stigma and empower others to seek help. By speaking out, you can help create a more supportive and informed environment for victims.

Breaking the cycle of financial abuse requires a concerted effort on multiple fronts. Victims must navigate a complex web of legal and societal barriers, while simultaneously rebuilding their financial lives and regaining their sense of self. It is a challenging journey, but one that can be undertaken with knowledge, support, and determination. By empowering ourselves and each other, we can create a world where financial abuse is no longer a hidden and accepted form of violence, but one that is recognized, addressed, and eradicated.

CHAPTER TWELVE

Assessing Your Financial Situation

❧

Before embarking on your journey to financial independence, it's crucial to assess your current financial situation honestly and comprehensively. This involves taking a deep dive into your finances, understanding your income, expenses, debts, and assets. This assessment will provide you with a clear picture of your starting point and help you develop a tailored plan for achieving financial freedom.

Start by gathering all relevant financial documents, including bank statements, credit card statements, loan documents, pay stubs, and any other financial records. These documents will provide you with detailed information about your income, expenses, and outstanding debts.

Next, create a detailed list of your monthly income sources. This includes your salary, any part-time work, alimony payments, child support, government assistance, and any other income streams. Be sure to include both regular and irregular income sources, such as bonuses, commissions, or gifts.

Following the income assessment, carefully analyze your monthly expenses. Categorize your expenses into essential needs like housing, utilities, groceries, transportation, and healthcare; discretionary spending like entertainment, dining, and shopping; and debt repayments, such as credit card bills, loan payments, and student loan payments. This detailed breakdown will help you identify areas where you can cut back on unnecessary expenses and prioritize your financial goals.

After evaluating your income and expenses, take stock of your assets and debts. Assets include your savings, investments, real estate, vehicles, and other valuable possessions. Debts include credit card balances, loans, student loans, and any other outstanding financial obligations.

It's essential to understand the specific terms of your debts, such as interest rates, repayment periods, and minimum payments. This information will help you strategize how to manage your debt effectively, potentially through debt consolidation, negotiating lower interest rates, or prioritizing payments on high-interest debts.

Once you've compiled a comprehensive list of your income, expenses, assets, and debts, you can calculate your net worth. This is the difference between your assets and liabilities. A positive net worth indicates that you have more assets than debts, while a negative net worth indicates that you owe more than you own.

Understanding your net worth can be a valuable tool for measuring your financial progress as you work towards regaining independence. It can also motivate you to develop strategies to increase your assets or reduce your debts.

Remember, this financial assessment is not about self-judgment or guilt. It's about gaining clarity and control over your financial life. Be honest with yourself about your situation, acknowledging both your strengths and areas for improvement. This assessment provides a solid foundation for developing a personalized financial plan that empowers you to break the cycle of financial abuse and build a financially secure future.

Developing a Budget

Creating a realistic budget is a cornerstone of financial stability. It helps you track your income and expenses, identify areas where you can save money, and allocate your resources effectively. A well-crafted budget is essential for managing your finances wisely and reaching your financial goals.

Start by using the detailed list of your income and expenses you created during the financial assessment. Divide your expenses into categories like housing, utilities, food, transportation, healthcare, debt repayments, and discretionary spending. This categorization will help you understand where your money is going and identify potential areas for cost-cutting.

Essential Expenses:
Housing:

This includes rent or mortgage payments, property taxes, insurance, and any associated fees.

Utilities:

This encompasses costs related to electricity, gas, water, internet, and phone service.

Food:

This category covers grocery bills, meals eaten out, and any other food- related expenses.

Transportation:

This includes car payments, gas, insurance, public transportation fares, and any other transportation costs.

Healthcare:

This category includes health insurance premiums, copays, and out-of- pocket medical expenses.

Discretionary Expenses:
Entertainment:

This covers costs related to movies, concerts, dining out, and any other leisure activities.

Shopping:

This includes clothing purchases, home goods, and any other retail spending.

Travel:

This covers expenses related to vacations, travel, and any other travel- related costs.

Subscriptions:

This category includes memberships, streaming services, and any other recurring subscriptions.

Debt Repayments:
Credit Card Bills:

This includes minimum payments and any additional payments towards outstanding balances.

Loan Payments:

This includes car loan payments, personal loan payments, and any other loan repayments.

Student Loan Payments:

This includes any outstanding student loan debt payments.

Tracking Your Spending

Once you've categorized your expenses, start tracking your spending diligently. Use a budgeting app, a spreadsheet, or a notebook to record every purchase you make. This will help you identify spending patterns and identify areas where you can cut back on unnecessary expenses.

Identifying Areas for Cost-Cutting

Review your spending categories and identify potential areas where you can cut back. For example, you may consider:

Reducing your housing costs:

This could involve finding a more affordable apartment, negotiating a lower rent, or moving in with roommates.

Negotiating lower utility rates:

Contact your utility providers to inquire about discounts or alternative plans.

Cooking more meals at home:

This can significantly reduce your food costs.

Finding cheaper transportation options:

Consider using public transportation, carpooling, or biking instead of driving alone.

Cutting back on unnecessary discretionary spending:

Review your entertainment, shopping, and travel expenses and identify areas where you can reduce spending.

Setting Financial Goals

Once you've created a budget and started tracking your spending, it's time to set financial goals. Having clear financial goals provides direction, motivation, and accountability.

Short-Term Goals (1-12 Months):
Build an emergency fund:

Aim to build a savings account that can cover three to six months of essential expenses.

Pay down high-interest debt:

Focus on paying down credit card debt or other high-interest loans as quickly as possible.

Save for a specific purchase:

This could be a down payment on a house, a new car, or a vacation.

Long-Term Goals (1+ Year):
Invest for retirement:

Consider investing in a retirement savings plan like a 401(k) or IRA.

Save for your children's education:

Start saving early for your children's college education.

Purchase a home:

Save for a down payment and explore different mortgage options.

Building Your Financial Literacy

Investing in your financial education is essential for managing your finances effectively. There are various resources available to help you gain a deeper understanding of personal finance.

Consider these options:

Taking online courses:

Many websites and institutions offer free or affordable courses on personal finance topics like budgeting, investing, and debt management.

Reading books and articles:

There are numerous books, magazines, and articles available that provide information and advice on personal finance.

Attending workshops and seminars:

Many community centers and financial institutions offer workshops and seminars on financial literacy.

The Importance of a Supportive Network

Building a strong support network is crucial for navigating the challenges of financial recovery. Consider seeking support from:

Family and friends:

Talk to trusted friends and family members about your situation. They can offer emotional support, practical assistance, and encouragement.

Support groups:

Connecting with others who have experienced financial abuse can provide valuable insights, empathy, and shared experiences.

Financial advisors:

A financial advisor can provide personalized guidance and support as you work towards financial stability.

Legal professionals:

If you're facing financial challenges due to legal issues, seeking legal advice is essential.

Remember, rebuilding your financial independence is a journey that requires patience, perseverance, and self-compassion. By taking these steps and building a strong support network, you can break the cycle of financial abuse and create a brighter financial future for yourself.

CHAPTER THIRTEEN

Creating A Financial Safety Plan

reating a financial safety plan is like building a sturdy bridge to a future free from financial control and manipulation. It's a proactive step to reclaim your economic autonomy and secure a path toward financial independence. While it might seem daunting, remember that you're not alone. You have the strength and ability to create a plan that empowers you to regain control of your financial life.

1. Take Stock of Your Current Financial Situation:

The first step is to gain a clear understanding of your current financial landscape. This involves honestly assessing your income, expenses, assets, and debts. It might feel overwhelming, but it's crucial for gaining a realistic perspective of your financial standing.

Income:

Begin by listing all sources of income, including salary, wages, benefits, child support, or any other financial assistance you receive.

Expenses:

Carefully track your monthly expenses, categorizing them into fixed expenses like rent, utilities, and loan payments, and variable expenses such as groceries, transportation, and entertainment.

Assets:

Identify your assets, which include any property you own, such as a house, car, savings accounts, investments, or valuable possessions.

Debts:

Make a list of all your outstanding debts, including the amount owed, interest rates, and monthly payments.

2. Secure Your Finances:

Now it's time to take steps to secure your finances. This involves protecting your assets and preventing further financial exploitation from the abuser.

Freezing Joint Accounts:

If you share bank accounts or credit cards with your abuser, it's crucial to take steps to prevent them from accessing your funds. Consider freezing or closing joint accounts. You may need to consult with a financial advisor or legal professional to understand the implications of such actions, especially if you are legally married or in a legal partnership.

Changing Passwords and PINs:

To protect your finances, change passwords for all online banking, credit card accounts, and any other financial platforms you use. Also, update your PINs for debit and credit cards.

Informing Credit Bureaus:

Contact the three major credit bureaus (Equifax, Experian, and TransUnion) and inform them about the situation. This helps prevent the abuser from opening new credit accounts in your name or taking out loans without your knowledge.

Monitoring Credit Reports:

It's important to regularly check your credit reports to ensure there are no fraudulent activities. You can obtain free credit reports annually from each credit bureau.

3. Creating a Budget and Financial Plan:

Once you have a clear picture of your current financial situation, you can start building a budget and financial plan. This helps you prioritize your spending, track your progress, and make informed financial decisions.

Prioritize Essential Expenses:

Focus on covering your essential expenses, such as housing, food, utilities, and transportation. This ensures you have the basic necessities covered.

Reduce Non-Essential Spending:

Review your expenses and identify areas where you can cut back on non- essential spending. For example, consider reducing dining out, entertainment, or subscriptions.

Seek Financial Support:

If you need assistance with housing, food, or other essential needs, explore resources available through community organizations, government assistance programs, and social services.

Consider a Financial Counselor:

Working with a certified financial counselor can provide guidance on budgeting, debt management, and building a financial plan that fits your needs and circumstances.

4. Building Financial Literacy:

Financial literacy is the key to making informed decisions about your money. Take the time to educate yourself about basic financial concepts, including:

Budgeting:

Understanding budgeting techniques, such as the 50/30/20 method, can help you allocate your income effectively.

Saving and Investing:

Learn the importance of saving and explore different investment options suitable for your financial goals.

Debt Management:

Gain knowledge about different debt repayment strategies, such as the snowball or avalanche method.

Credit Scores:

Understand how credit scores work and how to improve them.

5. Building a Network of Support:

Having a strong support network is essential during this time of financial recovery. Surround yourself with people who offer encouragement, guidance, and practical assistance.

Friends and Family:

Reach out to trusted friends and family members for emotional support and potential financial assistance.

Support Groups:

Connect with domestic violence support groups where you can share experiences, learn from others, and gain valuable insights.

Professional Services:

Seek assistance from professionals like social workers, counselors, financial advisors, and legal experts.

6. Setting Financial Goals:

Creating financial goals helps you stay motivated and focused on your financial independence. Set short-term and long-term goals, such as:

Short-Term Goals:

These could include building an emergency fund, paying off high-interest debts, or saving for a specific purchase.

Long-Term Goals:

Long-term goals may include purchasing a home, saving for retirement, or starting a business.

7. Celebrating Progress:

As you make progress toward your financial goals, acknowledge and celebrate your achievements. This helps build confidence and reinforces the positive changes you're making.

Financial Safety Plan Checklist:

Inventory:

Complete a thorough inventory of your income, expenses, assets, and debts.

Security:

Secure your finances by freezing joint accounts, changing passwords, and informing credit bureaus.

Budgeting:

Create a realistic budget that prioritizes essential expenses and reduces non- essential spending.

Financial Literacy:

Invest time in building your financial literacy by learning about budgeting, saving, investing, debt management, and credit scores.

Support Network:

Develop a strong support network of friends, family, support groups, and professional services.

Financial Goals:

Set realistic short-term and long-term financial goals to guide your progress.

Progress Celebration:

Acknowledge and celebrate your achievements along your journey toward financial independence.

Creating a financial safety plan is not about perfection; it's about taking consistent steps toward a brighter financial future. Remember, you're not alone, and there are resources available to help you along the way. By reclaiming your financial power, you are taking a powerful step toward a life free from abuse and toward the life you deserve.

CHAPTER FOURTEEN
Budgeting And Managing Resources

Regaining financial independence after experiencing financial abuse is a monumental task, demanding both practical strategies and emotional resilience. The first step in this journey is to assess your financial situation. This involves taking a hard look at your income, expenses, debts, and assets.

Many victims of financial abuse find themselves in a state of financial vulnerability, with limited access to funds or information about their own finances. If you are in this situation, it is crucial to start gathering as much information as possible. This might include:

Gathering financial documents:

This might include bank statements, credit card statements, loan agreements, tax returns, and any other paperwork that shows your income, expenses, and debts.

Identifying your assets:

Make a list of any assets you own, such as a home, a car, investments, or savings accounts.

Understanding your income and expenses:

Keep track of your income and expenses for a few months to understand your current financial standing. If you're unsure about your finances, consider reaching out to a financial advisor or a credit counselor for guidance.

Once you have a clear picture of your financial situation, you can start creating a financial safety plan. This plan will serve as a roadmap to guide you towards financial stability and independence.

CHAPTER FIFTEEN

Crafting A Financial Safety Plan:

A financial safety plan is a blueprint for securing your financial future. It includes steps like:

Opening a separate bank account:

This is essential to establish financial independence from your abuser. If possible, consider opening a joint account with a trusted friend or family member to help manage finances if you are feeling overwhelmed.

Securing your credit:

If your abuser has access to your credit cards or has taken out loans in your name, it is important to take steps to secure your credit. Contact your credit card companies and lenders to inform them of the situation and request a credit freeze or a change of account information. Consider using a credit monitoring service to keep track of your credit score and activity.

Seeking legal advice:

If you believe your abuser has committed financial fraud or identity theft, consult with an attorney to explore legal options.

Budgeting:

Create a realistic budget that outlines your income and expenses. This will help you prioritize essential expenses and identify areas where you can cut back on spending.

Saving:

Even small amounts saved consistently can build up over time and provide a financial cushion.

Debt management:

If you are struggling with debt, consider contacting a credit counselor or a debt consolidation service for help.

Developing a financial escape plan:

This plan should outline concrete steps you can take to leave an abusive relationship and achieve financial independence, including strategies for housing, transportation, employment, and childcare.

CHAPTER SIXTEEN

Budgeting And Managing Resources

Budgeting is a vital tool for achieving financial independence after financial abuse. By creating and sticking to a budget, you can gain control of your finances and prioritize your needs.

Creating a realistic budget:

This involves carefully tracking all your income and expenses. Keep detailed records of your income sources, such as salary, child support, or government benefits. Track your spending meticulously, breaking down your expenses into categories like housing, food, transportation, utilities, debt payments, and personal expenses.

Prioritizing essential expenses:

Focus on allocating enough funds to cover your essential needs, including housing, food, transportation, healthcare, and childcare. These expenses should be prioritized in your budget to ensure you have a safe and stable living situation.

Identifying areas for savings:

Look for areas where you can cut back on spending. This might involve reducing discretionary expenses, such as entertainment or dining out, or exploring more cost-effective options for necessities like groceries or utilities.

Finding affordable resources:

Take advantage of free or low-cost resources that can help manage your finances and reduce your expenses. These might include:

Community organizations:

Many local organizations offer free financial counseling, budgeting workshops, and support services to individuals experiencing financial hardship.

Government programs:

Explore federal, state, and local government programs that can provide financial assistance, such as food stamps, housing subsidies, or childcare assistance.

Free online resources:

Websites and online tools can help you create budgets, track expenses, and manage debt.

Exploring additional income sources :

Consider exploring additional income streams to increase your financial stability. This might include:

Part-time work:

Look for part-time jobs that fit your schedule and skills.

Freelancing:

Use your skills and talents to earn extra income through freelance work.

Selling unused items:

Declutter your home and sell items you no longer need through online marketplaces or consignment shops.

Starting a small business:

If you have an entrepreneurial spirit, consider starting a small business to generate income.

Using a budgeting app:

Numerous budgeting apps are available to help you track your expenses, create budgets, and set savings goals. These apps can provide insights into your spending habits and help you stay on track with your financial goals.

Building Financial Literacy And Skills:

❧

Financial literacy is essential for achieving long-term financial security and independence. By enhancing your understanding of financial concepts and building practical financial skills, you can empower yourself to make informed decisions about your finances.

Understanding financial concepts:

Take the time to understand basic financial concepts, such as budgeting, saving, investing, debt management, and credit scores. Numerous online resources, books, and workshops can help you acquire this knowledge.

Learning practical financial skills:

Developing practical financial skills, such as creating budgets, managing debt, and investing, is crucial. Consider taking courses, reading books, or attending workshops on these topics.

Seeking professional advice:

Don't hesitate to seek professional advice from financial experts, such as credit counselors, financial advisors, or tax professionals. They can provide personalized guidance and support tailored to your specific financial needs. ***Utilizing financial education resources:***

Take advantage of free or low-cost financial education resources available online and in your community. These resources can help you learn about money management, credit, investing, and other financial topics.

CHAPTER EIGHTEEN

Creating A Network Of Support And Resources

Building a supportive network of individuals and organizations can provide invaluable assistance as you embark on your journey to financial independence.

Reaching out to trusted friends and family:

Share your situation with trusted friends and family members who can offer emotional support and practical help. They can provide a listening ear, offer encouragement, and help you access resources.

Connecting with support groups:

Join support groups for victims of domestic violence or financial abuse. These groups provide a safe and supportive environment for sharing experiences, learning from others, and receiving encouragement.

Seeking professional help:

Don't hesitate to seek professional help from therapists, counselors, or financial advisors. These professionals can provide guidance, support, and resources tailored to your needs.

Contacting community organizations:

Many local community organizations offer services and programs designed to support victims of domestic violence and financial abuse. These organizations can provide financial assistance, legal aid, housing assistance, and other resources to help you get back on your feet.

Remember, regaining financial independence is a process that takes time and effort. Be patient with yourself and celebrate every step you take towards your goals. With dedication, perseverance, and the right resources, you can break free from the chains of financial abuse and create a secure and prosperous future for yourself and your family.

CHAPTER NINETEEN

Building Financial Literacy and Skills

❧

Financial literacy is the foundation of financial independence, and regaining control over your finances is crucial after experiencing financial abuse. It empowers you to make informed decisions, manage your money effectively, and build a secure financial future. Enhancing your financial literacy and acquiring essential financial skills will be a journey, but it's a journey worth taking. This journey involves understanding basic financial concepts, developing budgeting and saving habits, and learning how to navigate the financial world confidently.

Understanding the Basics:

Start by grasping fundamental financial concepts like budgeting, saving, debt management, and investing. There are numerous free resources available online and in libraries, such as articles, videos, and interactive tools. Websites like Khan Academy, Investopedia, and the U.S. Securities and Exchange Commission offer comprehensive information on personal finance. These resources can help you understand:

Budgeting:

Creating a budget involves tracking your income and expenses to understand where your money goes. This allows you to identify areas where you can cut back on unnecessary spending and allocate funds for your financial goals.

Saving:

Developing a savings plan is essential for achieving financial security. Setting aside a portion of your income regularly helps you build an emergency fund, save for future expenses like a house down payment or education, and reduce dependence on others for financial support.

Debt Management:

Understanding different types of debt, such as credit card debt, student loans, and personal loans, and learning effective strategies for managing and paying them off is crucial. Creating a debt repayment plan can help you prioritize debt and work towards becoming debt-free.

Investing:

Investing is a powerful tool for growing your wealth over time. You can explore different investment options, like stocks, bonds, mutual funds, and real estate, based on your risk tolerance and financial goals. Investing can help you secure your future and create financial independence.

Developing Practical Skills:

Once you have a grasp of the basics, it's time to develop practical financial skills. Here are some essential skills to acquire:

Financial Record Keeping:

Maintain accurate records of your income, expenses, and debts. This allows you to monitor your financial progress, identify patterns in your spending, and make informed financial decisions. Keeping track of your finances will also help you understand your financial situation and create a realistic budget.

Negotiation and Communication:

Developing strong negotiation and communication skills can be invaluable in your financial journey. Whether it's negotiating with creditors to lower interest rates, communicating with landlords about rent payments, or negotiating with financial institutions for better loan terms, these skills empower you to stand up for your financial well-being.

Credit Management:

Understanding how credit works and managing your credit effectively is critical for financial security. This includes knowing your credit score, understanding how it's calculated, and using credit responsibly to build a positive credit history. Good credit can open doors to lower interest rates, better loan terms, and more favorable financial opportunities.

Financial Planning:

Creating a long-term financial plan is essential for achieving your financial goals. This plan should include your short-term and long-term financial goals, strategies for achieving them, and a roadmap for managing your finances effectively. A financial plan provides clarity and direction in your financial journey, guiding you towards financial independence.

Tools and Resources for Financial Empowerment:

There are numerous tools and resources available to support your financial empowerment journey. Explore these to enhance your understanding and gain practical skills:

Budgeting Apps and Software:

Utilize budgeting apps and software to simplify tracking your income and expenses. These apps often provide personalized financial insights and guidance, helping you make informed spending decisions and stay on track with your financial goals.

Financial Education Websites:

Websites like the Consumer Financial Protection Bureau (CFPB), the Federal Trade Commission (FTC), and the National Endowment for Financial Education (NEFE) offer valuable resources and educational materials on various financial topics.

Local Financial Literacy Programs:

Explore local community centers, libraries, and financial institutions that offer financial education programs and workshops. These programs can provide hands-on learning experiences and connect you with experts who can offer personalized guidance.

Financial Counseling Services:

If you're struggling to manage your finances or need personalized advice, consider seeking guidance from a certified financial counselor. These professionals can help you create a budget, develop a debt repayment plan, and navigate complex financial situations.

Financial Literacy Books and Articles:

Read books and articles from reputable authors and financial experts to gain a deeper understanding of financial concepts, strategies, and best practices. These resources can provide valuable insights and practical tips for managing your finances effectively.

The Importance of Financial Independence:

Gaining financial independence is not only about money; it's about empowerment. When you have control over your finances, you have control over your life. It provides a sense of security, reduces dependence on others, and allows you to pursue your dreams and goals without financial limitations.

Financial independence is a process, not a destination. It requires consistent effort, commitment to learning, and the willingness to break free from financial abuse's grip.

Remember, you are not alone on this journey. There are resources and support systems available to guide you every step of the way. By building your financial literacy and acquiring essential financial skills, you are taking control of your future and building a foundation for a brighter, more secure tomorrow.

CHAPTER TWENTY

Creating A Network Of Support And Resources

Rebuilding your life after financial abuse can be a daunting task, but it's important to remember that you are not alone. One of the most crucial steps you can take is to create a supportive network of individuals and resources that can provide guidance, encouragement, and practical assistance. This network will become your lifeline as you navigate the complexities of reclaiming your financial independence.

Building Your Support System

The first step in creating a network is to identify the individuals who can offer emotional support and practical help. These individuals may include:

Family and Friends:

Reach out to trusted family members and friends who have a history of supporting you. Let them know what you're going through and what kind of help you need. Even if they don't have financial expertise, their emotional support and understanding can be invaluable.

Therapist or Counselor:

A therapist or counselor can provide a safe and confidential space to process your experiences, work through emotional trauma, and develop healthy coping mechanisms. They can also help you identify and address any underlying issues that may be contributing to your financial vulnerability.

Support Groups:

Connecting with others who have experienced similar situations can be incredibly empowering. Support groups for survivors of domestic violence or financial abuse can provide a sense of community, shared understanding, and practical advice.

Domestic Violence Advocates:

Domestic violence advocates are trained professionals who can provide legal information, safety planning, and resources for victims of abuse. They can help you navigate the legal system, understand your rights, and access essential services.

Accessing Resources for Financial Independence

Once you have built your support network, you can start exploring the wealth of resources available to help you achieve financial independence. These resources include:

Financial Counseling:

Financial counselors can provide personalized guidance on budgeting, debt management, and financial planning. They can help you assess your financial situation, develop a budget, and create a plan for paying off debts.

Legal Aid Organizations:

Legal aid organizations provide free or low-cost legal assistance to individuals who cannot afford an attorney. They can help you understand your legal rights and options, negotiate with creditors, and seek legal protection from your abuser.

Government Assistance Programs:

There are several government assistance programs that can provide financial aid, housing assistance, and other essential services. These programs may be available to victims of domestic violence, low-income families, and individuals with disabilities.

Nonprofit Organizations:

Nonprofit organizations dedicated to supporting victims of domestic violence often offer a range of resources, including financial assistance, housing assistance, counseling, and job training programs.

Community Resources:

Many communities offer free or low-cost resources, such as food banks, clothing banks, and job training programs, that can help victims of domestic violence meet their basic needs.

Navigating Financial Institutions and Legal Processes

It is important to understand your rights and options when dealing with financial institutions and legal processes.

Freezing Accounts:

If you believe your abuser has access to your accounts, you may be able to freeze them to prevent further misuse.

Changing Passwords and PINs:

Immediately change the passwords and PINs for all your accounts, including bank accounts, credit cards, online services, and social media accounts.

Filing Restraining Orders:

If you are in danger, you can file a restraining order to legally prevent your abuser from contacting you or coming near you.

Reporting Financial Abuse to Authorities:

Financial abuse is a crime, and you have the right to report it to the authorities. Reporting can help protect other potential victims and hold your abuser accountable.

Creating a Financial Escape Plan

Developing a financial escape plan is essential for securing your future. This plan should include:

Assessing your current financial situation:

This includes identifying your income, expenses, assets, and debts.

Setting realistic financial goals:

Focus on achievable short-term goals and long-term goals that will provide financial security.

Creating a budget:

A budget will help you track your income and expenses and identify areas where you can save money.

Developing a debt management strategy:

This may involve negotiating with creditors to reduce your debt, consolidating your debt, or seeking debt relief programs.

Seeking financial literacy resources:

There are numerous online resources and books available to help you improve your financial literacy and understanding.

Building Financial Confidence and Security

Rebuilding your financial life after abuse is a journey that requires patience, resilience, and a commitment to building financial confidence and security. Remember:

You are not alone:

There are people who care about you and want to help you. Reach out to your support network and seek help from professionals.

You deserve financial freedom:

Financial abuse is a form of control and manipulation. You have the right to control your finances and build a secure financial future.

It's a process, not a sprint:

It may take time to rebuild your financial life, but every small step forward is a victory.

Celebrate your progress:

Acknowledge and celebrate your successes along the way. This will help you stay motivated and focused on your goals.

By creating a supportive network, accessing available resources, and developing a financial escape plan, you can regain control of your finances, rebuild your life, and create a future free from financial abuse.

CHAPTER TWENTY ONE

Confronting Emotional Barriers

The road to financial freedom after experiencing financial abuse is paved with more than just numbers and budgets. It's a journey that demands confronting the emotional scars left behind, the deep-seated fears, and the shattered self-confidence. Imagine a survivor, let's call her Sarah, finally escaping an abusive relationship. She's free, but the echoes of his control linger. Sarah battles with self-doubt, blaming herself for the financial mess she's in. This emotional turmoil can be a formidable obstacle, hindering her ability to move forward.

This is where the crucial work of healing begins, a journey inward that often parallels the external efforts of rebuilding finances. It's about addressing the core beliefs that have been warped by the abuse, and re- framing those narratives to reflect a sense of empowerment and self-worth.

The first step is acknowledging the emotional impact of financial abuse. The experience can leave a trail of emotional wreckage. Victims often grapple with feelings of shame, guilt, and a profound lack of self-worth. The abuser's constant criticism and belittling can erode one's confidence, making it difficult to trust their own judgment. Sarah, for example, constantly second-guesses her every financial decision, paralyzed by the fear of making a mistake. The emotional burden of financial abuse can manifest in various ways:

Anxiety and Stress:

The constant fear of financial instability, the pressure to please the abuser, and the uncertainty about the future can lead to crippling anxiety and stress. Sleepless nights, racing thoughts, and a constant sense of unease can become the norm.

Depression and Low Self-Esteem:

Financial abuse often goes hand-in-hand with emotional and psychological abuse. The abuser's constant criticism, manipulation, and control can take a toll on one's self-esteem, leading to feelings of worthlessness and hopelessness. This can manifest as depression, withdrawal, and a lack of motivation to pursue goals.

Trauma and Post-Traumatic Stress Disorder (PTSD):

The experience of financial abuse can be deeply traumatic, leaving lasting emotional scars. Symptoms of PTSD, such as flashbacks, nightmares, and emotional numbness, can be a significant obstacle to healing and recovery.

Fear and Distrust:

After experiencing financial abuse, victims often struggle with fear and distrust, not just of the abuser but also of other people and financial institutions. This can lead to avoidance of financial planning, a reluctance to seek help, and a sense of isolation. Confronting these emotional barriers requires a multi-faceted approach:

Therapy and Counseling:

Professional therapy can provide a safe and supportive environment to process the trauma of financial abuse. A therapist can help individuals identify their emotional triggers, develop coping mechanisms, and build healthy coping skills. This can be crucial in managing anxiety, stress, and depression, allowing survivors to confront the emotional baggage and begin to heal.

Support Groups and Networks:

Joining support groups or connecting with other survivors can offer a sense of community and shared understanding. Sharing stories, offering advice, and simply knowing that others have gone through similar experiences can be profoundly validating and empowering.

Self-Care and Mindfulness:

Prioritizing self-care activities like exercise, meditation, or engaging in hobbies can be crucial for emotional well-being. Engaging in activities that bring joy and a sense of accomplishment can help rebuild self-esteem and counter the negative self-talk often associated with financial abuse.

Setting Boundaries:

Re-establishing boundaries with others is essential for emotional and financial recovery. This might involve setting limits on how much personal information is shared, learning to say "no" to requests that feel uncomfortable, and building a support network that respects these boundaries.

Sarah, with the support of a therapist and a supportive friend, starts to understand the psychological tactics the abuser used. She acknowledges that she wasn't responsible for his financial irresponsibility. She reclaims her power by creating a budget, focusing on her own needs, and taking control of her finances.

It's important to remember that there is no one-size-fits-all approach to overcoming the emotional barriers associated with financial abuse. The journey is unique for every individual. However, by taking the time to address the emotional wounds, survivors can equip themselves to navigate the complexities of financial recovery, building a brighter future free from the shadows of past abuse.

Remember, you are not alone. There are resources and support systems available to help you navigate this challenging journey.

With the right support and commitment to healing, it is possible to overcome the emotional barriers and build a strong, independent financial foundation.

CHAPTER TWENTY TWO

Reclaiming Self Esteem And Identity

The journey of healing from financial abuse is not just about regaining financial stability; it's also about reclaiming your self-esteem and rebuilding your sense of identity. You have been through an incredibly challenging experience, and it's natural to feel lost, confused, and unsure of who you are. The abuser's tactics have likely chipped away at your confidence, making you doubt your abilities and worth. But know this: you are not defined by the abuse. You are strong, capable, and worthy of love and respect.

The first step in reclaiming your self-esteem is acknowledging the impact of the abuse. It's crucial to understand that the financial control and manipulation you endured were not your fault. You were a victim of a powerful, manipulative force. It's essential to release the guilt and shame that you may be carrying.

Many survivors find it helpful to engage in self-reflection and journaling. Writing down your thoughts and feelings can help you process the trauma and gain a clearer perspective. It can be an effective way to identify the negative self-beliefs that have taken root. These could include:

"I am not good enough."

"I am incapable of making good decisions." "I am a burden to others."

Once you identify these negative self-beliefs, you can start to challenge them. Replace them with positive affirmations that affirm your worth and capabilities.

"I am strong and resilient."

"I am capable of making wise choices." "I am deserving of happiness and love."

Remember, these affirmations are not just empty words; they are tools to retrain your brain and reprogram your thought patterns.

Another crucial step in rebuilding your self-esteem is to reconnect with your passions and interests. What activities bring you joy? What hobbies did you neglect during the abuse? Re-engaging in these activities can help you rediscover your identity and reconnect with your inner self. You might find solace in creative pursuits like writing, painting, or music. Perhaps you find joy in physical activity or exploring nature.

It's also essential to nurture your social connections. Surround yourself with supportive friends and family members who believe in you and your potential. Seek out support groups or online communities where you can connect with other survivors and share your experiences. You are not alone in this journey.

Developing a strong support network is crucial for your emotional and psychological well-being. It allows you to feel heard, validated, and understood. It also helps you to build a sense of community and belonging, reminding you that you are not alone in your journey.

As you rebuild your self-esteem and identity, remember that it is a process. It will take time and effort, but the rewards are worth it. You will emerge from this experience stronger, wiser, and more empowered. Trust in your ability to heal and reclaim your life.

Learning to Trust Yourself

Trust is fundamental to a healthy sense of self-esteem. It is the ability to believe in yourself, your decisions, and your abilities. Unfortunately, financial abuse often erodes trust. It creates a sense of vulnerability and helplessness. The abuser might have intentionally undermined your judgment and made you doubt your own thoughts.

Rebuilding trust in yourself requires a commitment to re-examining your relationship with yourself and the world around you. It is about relearning to listen to your intuition, acknowledge your needs, and act on your own behalf.

Here are some steps to rebuild trust in yourself:

1. Pay attention to your gut feelings.

When making decisions, take the time to listen to your intuition. It is your inner voice, offering you guidance and wisdom. Trust your gut feeling, even if it differs from what others may suggest.

2. Seek out healthy relationships.

Surround yourself with people who genuinely care for you and support you. Build relationships based on mutual respect, honesty, and authenticity. These relationships will foster a sense of safety and trust.

3. Be kind and forgiving towards yourself.

Recognize that mistakes are part of life. Learn from them and move forward with compassion and understanding. Remember that you are human, and it is okay to make mistakes.

4. Celebrate your achievements.

Recognize and celebrate your successes, no matter how small they may seem. Acknowledge your strength, resilience, and progress.

5. Practice self-care.

Prioritize activities that nourish your body, mind, and spirit. This could include exercise,

meditation, spending time in nature, or engaging in hobbies that you enjoy.

6. Set realistic goals.

Don't overwhelm yourself with overly ambitious goals. Instead, focus on setting small, achievable goals that you can work towards gradually.

7. Seek professional help.

If you are struggling to rebuild trust in yourself or if the emotional impact of the abuse is overwhelming, consider seeking the guidance of a therapist or counselor. They can provide you with tools and strategies to navigate the journey to recovery.

Embracing Your Strengths and Passions

After the trauma of financial abuse, you might feel adrift, uncertain about your passions, and unsure of your path forward. It is common to feel a sense of disconnect from yourself. But this is an opportunity to rediscover your true self and embrace your strengths and passions.

Here are some strategies to help you embrace your strengths and passions:

1. Take stock of your skills and talents.

Reflect on your past experiences and accomplishments. Identify the skills and talents you possess, even if you haven't had a chance to use them lately. What did you excel at? What activities brought you a sense of fulfillment?

2. Explore new possibilities.

Be open to new experiences and explore different areas of interest. Take a class, attend a workshop, or volunteer in a field that excites you.

Remember that your passions may evolve over time, so allow yourself to explore and discover new paths.

3. Set aside time for your passions.

It's easy to get caught up in the day-to-day grind, but it's essential to make time for your passions. Even if it's just for an hour a week, dedicate time to engage in activities that bring you joy.

4. Don't be afraid to take risks.

Stepping outside of your comfort zone can be daunting, but it can also lead to exciting discoveries and opportunities. Embrace challenges and allow yourself to grow and learn.

5. Find mentors and role models.

Seek out individuals who inspire you and whose journeys resonate with you. They can offer guidance, support, and a different perspective.

6. Celebrate your progress.

Recognize and acknowledge your efforts and accomplishments. It is essential to celebrate your growth and milestones along the way.

Remember, it's okay to be unsure or to feel lost at times. The process of rebuilding your life can be challenging. But by actively pursuing your passions and embracing your strengths, you will gradually rediscover your purpose and direction.

The Power of Self-Compassion

Self-compassion is crucial during the healing process. It is about treating yourself with kindness, understanding, and acceptance, especially during moments of struggle.

Financial abuse can leave you feeling inadequate, ashamed, and guilty. You might blame yourself for the abuse or question your own judgment. But it is essential to remember that you are not to blame. You are worthy of love and compassion.

Practice self-compassion by:

1. Being kind to yourself.

Instead of criticizing yourself, offer yourself words of encouragement and support. Remember that you are human and that making mistakes is part of the process.

2. Acknowledging your feelings.

Allow yourself to experience your emotions fully, without judgment or suppression. Don't try to bottle up your feelings. Give yourself permission to feel sad, angry, or scared.

3. Remembering that you are not alone.

Financial abuse is a widespread issue. Millions of individuals have experienced similar challenges. Connect with support groups or online communities to remind yourself that you are not alone in your journey.

4. Forgiving yourself.

Let go of the guilt and shame you may be carrying. You deserve to forgive

yourself for the mistakes you made or for the things you didn't do during the abuse. Remember, you were in a difficult situation, and you did the best you could.

5. Prioritizing self-care.

Make time for activities that nourish your body, mind, and spirit. This could include getting enough sleep, eating healthy foods, exercising regularly, spending time in nature, or engaging in hobbies that you enjoy.

6. Seeking professional help.

If you are struggling to practice self-compassion or if the emotional impact of the abuse is overwhelming, consider seeking the guidance of a therapist or counselor. They can provide you with tools and strategies for navigating the journey to recovery.

Self-compassion is not about being complacent or self-indulgent. It is about treating yourself with kindness and understanding, the same way you would treat a loved one who is going through a challenging time. It is a powerful tool for healing, growth, and self-acceptance.

Rebuilding Your Identity

Financial abuse can have a profound impact on your sense of identity. The abuser may have attempted to control your finances, limit your opportunities, and undermine your self-confidence, making you feel trapped and dependent. As a result, you may have lost sight of your values, passions, and goals.

Rebuilding your identity is a process of self-discovery and rediscovery. It involves exploring your values, beliefs, and aspirations.

Here are some steps to help you rebuild your identity:

1. Reconnect with your core values.

What matters most to you? What beliefs guide your decisions and actions? Reflect on your values and prioritize those that are most important to you.

2. Identify your strengths and talents.

What are you good at? What skills do you possess? Think about your past experiences and accomplishments. Identify areas where you excel.

3. Explore your interests and passions.

What activities bring you joy? What hobbies did you neglect during the abuse? Re-engage in these activities or explore new ones that spark your interest.

4. Set goals and make plans.

What do you want to achieve in your life? Set goals, both big and small, that align with your values and passions. Make plans to work towards these goals.

5. Be patient and kind to yourself.

Rebuilding your identity takes time and effort. Be patient with yourself and celebrate your progress along the way.

6. Seek support.

Connect with others who understand the challenges of rebuilding your life after abuse. Support groups, online communities, and trusted friends and family can offer encouragement and guidance.

As you reclaim your identity, remember that you are unique and valuable. You have the power to define your own path and create the life you desire. The journey may be challenging, but it is also an opportunity for personal growth, transformation, and empowerment.

CHAPTER TWENTY THREE

Navigating Legal Systems And Protections

❧

The legal system offers a crucial safety net for victims of financial abuse, providing a framework for seeking justice and protecting their rights.

Understanding these legal avenues is paramount to reclaiming control and achieving financial independence. Navigating the legal system can feel overwhelming and intimidating, particularly for those who have been isolated and controlled by an abuser. This chapter aims to demystify legal protections available to victims of financial abuse, empowering you to assert your rights and seek redress for the financial injustices you may have endured.

Understanding Your Rights

Every jurisdiction has laws designed to safeguard victims of financial abuse and address the complex dynamics of these cases. The first step in navigating legal systems is to understand your rights. It is essential to know that financial abuse is a recognized form of domestic violence and carries legal consequences for perpetrators.

Domestic Violence Laws:

Laws pertaining to domestic violence often extend to encompass financial abuse. This means that victims can seek legal protection and remedies, even if the abuse is solely financial.

Financial Abuse Laws:

Specific laws may address financial abuse, such as those relating to:

Fraud and Identity Theft:

These laws address cases where the abuser misrepresents their financial status, takes out loans or credit cards in the victim's name without their consent, or uses stolen information to gain financial advantage.

Embezzlement and Theft:

Laws against embezzlement and theft apply when the abuser steals money, assets, or property belonging to the victim.

Financial Exploitation of Vulnerable Adults:

In cases involving seniors or individuals with disabilities, specialized laws may be in place to protect them from financial exploitation by abusers.

Civil Orders of Protection:

These orders can be obtained from a court to prohibit an abuser from taking specific actions, such as contacting the victim, accessing their accounts, or coming near their residence or workplace. Civil orders of protection can be critical for safeguarding your financial and physical safety.

Seeking Legal Assistance

Legal aid and advocacy organizations offer invaluable support to victims of financial abuse. They provide information about your rights, help navigate legal processes, and often represent victims pro bono or at a reduced cost.

Legal Aid Services:

Legal aid programs offer free or low-cost legal assistance to individuals with limited financial resources.

Domestic Violence Legal Advocacy Groups:

These organizations specialize in representing victims of domestic violence, including those facing financial abuse.

Pro Bono Attorneys:

Many lawyers offer pro bono (free) legal services to individuals who cannot afford legal representation.

Gathering Evidence:

A critical aspect of legal proceedings is presenting evidence to support your claims of financial abuse. Collecting evidence can be challenging, especially if the abuser has hidden assets or manipulated financial records.

Financial Documents:

Gather copies of bank statements, credit card bills, loan agreements, tax returns, property deeds, insurance policies, and any other documents that show the abuser's financial activities and any evidence of financial control.

Correspondence and Communication:

Keep copies of emails, texts, letters, and voicemails that demonstrate financial manipulation, threats, or control.

Witnesses:

If possible, identify witnesses who can testify about the abuser's financial behavior and your experience of financial abuse.

Legal Options and Remedies

Depending on the nature and severity of the financial abuse, various legal options may be available.

Criminal Charges:

If the abuse involves crimes like theft, fraud, or embezzlement, the perpetrator may face criminal charges, leading to potential jail time and fines.

Civil Lawsuits:

Victims can pursue civil lawsuits to seek financial compensation for damages resulting from the abuse.

Protective Orders:

As mentioned earlier, civil orders of protection can provide immediate legal safeguards against further abuse.

Divorce Proceedings:

If the abuser is a spouse, divorce proceedings can address financial issues related to asset division and spousal support.

Moving Forward with Confidence

The legal system can be a valuable tool for rebuilding financial security after abuse. It offers protection, recourse, and a means to hold abusers accountable. However, it is essential to remember that the legal process can be lengthy and emotionally draining.

Here are some tips for navigating the legal system with confidence:

Seek Support:

Connect with a therapist or counselor who specializes in domestic violence and financial abuse. Their expertise can provide emotional support and coping strategies as you navigate legal proceedings.

Educate Yourself:

Research laws and legal options relevant to your situation. The more you understand your rights, the more empowered you will feel.

Be Patient:

Legal processes often take time. Be prepared for delays and unexpected challenges.

Focus on Your Goals:

Remember that the goal of legal action is to reclaim your financial autonomy, safety, and peace of mind.

Conclusion:

Navigating legal systems and seeking justice can be a

daunting task, but it is not insurmountable. By understanding your rights, gathering evidence, seeking legal assistance, and focusing on your goals, you can take steps toward regaining financial control and rebuilding a secure future. Remember that you are not alone. Legal professionals, support groups, and advocacy organizations are dedicated to assisting victims of financial abuse.

CHAPTER TWENTY FOUR

The Role Of Therapy And Counseling

The journey to overcome financial abuse is multifaceted and requires a holistic approach to healing. While practical strategies for regaining financial independence are crucial, addressing the emotional and psychological scars left behind is equally vital. This is where therapy and counseling play a pivotal role, providing a safe and supportive space for individuals to process their experiences, rebuild their confidence, and ultimately find a path toward emotional well-being.

Financial abuse, as a form of domestic violence, leaves lasting emotional and psychological wounds. Victims often grapple with feelings of shame, guilt, self-doubt, and fear. They may struggle to trust their instincts, make decisions independently, or even believe that they deserve financial stability. Therapy and counseling offer a structured and empathetic environment to explore these complex emotions and navigate the path to healing.

The Benefits of Therapy and Counseling

Therapy and counseling provide several benefits for individuals recovering from financial abuse:

Processing Trauma:

Financial abuse, like all forms of abuse, can be deeply traumatic. Therapy provides a safe and supportive space to process these traumatic experiences without judgment. It allows individuals to express their emotions, confront their fears, and work through the emotional fallout of financial abuse.

Building Self-Esteem:

Financial abuse often targets a victim's self-worth and self-confidence. Therapy can help individuals reclaim their sense of self-worth and rebuild their confidence in their ability to manage their finances and make independent decisions.

Challenging Negative Beliefs:

Financial abuse can instill negative beliefs about oneself, money, and relationships. Therapy helps individuals identify and challenge these limiting beliefs, replacing them with healthier and more empowering perspectives.

Developing Healthy Boundaries:

Financial abuse often involves the breakdown of healthy boundaries. Therapy empowers individuals to establish clear and healthy boundaries, both in their relationships and in their financial lives, to prevent future exploitation.

Improving Communication Skills:

Financial abuse can damage communication within relationships. Therapy helps individuals develop assertive communication skills, enabling them to express their needs and concerns effectively.

Creating a Safety Plan:

Therapy can play a crucial role in creating a safety plan for individuals leaving an abusive relationship. This plan can encompass both financial and emotional aspects, ensuring that the individual has the resources and support they need to transition safely and rebuild their lives.

Developing Coping Mechanisms:

Financial abuse can lead to stress, anxiety, and depression. Therapy helps individuals develop healthy coping mechanisms to manage their emotions, reduce stress, and build resilience in the face of future challenges.

Finding Support and Connection:

Therapy provides a supportive and non-judgmental space where

individuals can connect with a therapist who understands their experiences and offers encouragement and guidance.

Types of Therapy for Financial Abuse:

There are various types of therapy that can be beneficial for survivors of financial abuse:

Individual Therapy:

This type of therapy focuses on the individual's unique experiences and provides a safe space to process emotions, build self-esteem, and develop healthy coping mechanisms.

Group Therapy:

Group therapy offers a sense of community and connection with others who have experienced similar trauma. It allows individuals to share their stories, learn from each other's experiences, and gain support from peers.

Trauma-Informed Therapy:

This approach recognizes the impact of trauma on the individual's mental and emotional well-being. It focuses on helping individuals understand and process their traumatic experiences in a safe and supportive environment.

Cognitive Behavioral Therapy (CBT):

CBT helps individuals identify and challenge negative thoughts and behaviors associated with financial abuse. It focuses on developing more adaptive thought patterns and behaviors to manage stress, anxiety, and depression.

Dialectical Behavior Therapy (DBT):

DBT focuses on developing emotional regulation skills, distress tolerance, and interpersonal effectiveness. It can be particularly helpful for individuals who experience intense emotions or struggle with self-harm behaviors.

Finding the Right Therapist

Finding a qualified and experienced therapist who understands the nuances of financial abuse is crucial. Here are some tips for finding the right therapist:

Seek referrals:

Ask friends, family members, or trusted professionals for recommendations.

Check therapist credentials:

Look for therapists with specialized training in domestic violence, financial abuse, or trauma-informed therapy.

Consider the therapist's approach:

Choose a therapist whose approach aligns with your personal preferences and needs.

Schedule an initial consultation:

Use this time to discuss your concerns, ask questions, and determine if the therapist is a good fit for you.

Challenges in Seeking Therapy

Despite the immense benefits of therapy, seeking help can be challenging for survivors of financial abuse:

Financial Constraints:

Therapy can be expensive, and individuals recovering from financial abuse may face financial limitations.

Stigma:

There can be a stigma associated with seeking mental health support, leading some individuals to feel ashamed or hesitant to seek therapy. **Fear of Judgment:**

Victims of financial abuse may fear being judged or disbelieved by a therapist.

Lack of Trust:

Past experiences with abuse can make it difficult for victims to trust a therapist or open up about their experiences.

Accessing Resources:

Finding a therapist who understands financial abuse and is accessible to victims may be difficult depending on location and resources available.

Overcoming Barriers to Therapy

Overcoming these barriers is essential for accessing the healing power of therapy:

Explore low-cost or free options:

Look for community mental health centers, sliding scale therapists, or free support groups.

Reach out to advocacy organizations:

Many organizations provide resources and referrals for affordable or free therapy services.

Educate yourself:

Learn about the benefits of therapy and the importance of seeking help for emotional well-being.

Build a support system:

Surround yourself with trusted friends, family members, or support groups who can provide encouragement and understanding.

Therapy and counseling are powerful tools for healing from the emotional and psychological effects of financial abuse. It is a journey that requires patience, dedication, and a willingness to confront the past and embrace a brighter future. Remember, seeking help is a sign of strength, not weakness. By embracing the benefits of therapy, individuals can begin to rebuild their lives and find lasting peace and freedom.

CHAPTER TWENTY FIVE

Setting New Goals For A Secure Future

The journey to reclaiming your financial security after experiencing financial abuse is about more than just balancing budgets and building savings. It's about rebuilding your confidence, reclaiming your power, and charting a new course for a future free from control and manipulation.

It's time to set your sights on the horizon and envision the life you want to create. Remember, your financial freedom is not a distant dream – it's a tangible goal within your reach. To achieve it, we need to work together, step by step, to build a solid foundation for your financial security. This chapter will guide you through the process of setting realistic and attainable goals, empowering you to take control of your financial future.

Let's start with the basics:

Identify Your Needs and Desires.

This might seem straightforward, but it's crucial. Take some time to reflect on your dreams, your aspirations, and your basic needs. Ask yourself:

What are your priorities for the future?

What are your goals for financial independence? What kind of lifestyle do you envision for yourself?

What are your basic needs for housing, food, transportation, and healthcare?

This process of self-reflection is essential. It will help you define your financial goals and create a plan that aligns with your values and your vision of a secure future.

Once you have a clear understanding of your needs and desires, you can start:

Setting Specific, Measurable, Achievable, Relevant, and Time-Bound (SMART) Goals.

This framework provides structure and focus as you map out your financial journey.

Specific:

Your goals should be clearly defined, leaving no room for ambiguity. Instead of saying "I want to save more money," try "I want to save $500 per month for the next six months."

Measurable:

Goals should be quantifiable, allowing you to track progress and celebrate milestones.

Achievable:

While ambitious is good, setting goals that are unrealistic can lead to discouragement. Break down large goals into smaller, manageable steps. **Relevant:**

Your goals should align with your needs and values. Ensure that they are meaningful to you and support your overall financial well-being.

Time-Bound:

Establish deadlines for your goals, creating a sense of urgency and motivation.

Examples of SMART Financial Goals:
Saving Goal:

"I will save $100 per week for the next year to create an emergency fund of

$5,200."

Debt Reduction Goal:

"I will pay off my $3,000 credit card debt within the next 18 months by making an extra $100 payment each month."

Investment Goal:

"I will invest $200 per month in a low-cost index fund for the next five years."

Housing Goal:

"I will secure a safe and affordable apartment within the next six months by working with a housing counselor and exploring rental assistance programs."

Education Goal:

"I will enroll in a vocational training program within the next year to enhance my job skills and increase my earning potential." As you set your goals, be sure to consider your

Current Financial Situation.

This involves honestly assessing your income, expenses, assets, and debts.

Income:

Identify all sources of income, both regular and irregular, such as wages, benefits, and any other financial support you receive.

Expenses:

Track your monthly expenses, categorizing them into essential (housing, utilities, food, transportation) and non-essential (entertainment, dining out, subscriptions).

Assets:

Make a list of your assets, including cash, savings, investments, property, and any valuable possessions.

Debts:

Identify all debts, including credit card balances, student loans, medical bills, and any outstanding personal loans.

Creating a Budget:

A budget is an essential tool for financial planning and management. It provides a clear picture of your income and expenses, allowing you to allocate funds effectively and track progress towards your goals.

There are various budgeting methods to choose from, and you can explore different options to find what works best for you:

50/30/20 Budget:

This method allocates 50% of your income to needs, 30% to wants, and 20% to savings and debt repayment.

Zero-Based Budgeting:

This method requires you to allocate every dollar of your income to specific categories, ensuring that you account for every expense.

Envelope Budgeting:

This method involves dividing your income into categories and placing cash into separate envelopes for each category.

Digital Budgeting Apps:

Various apps are available to help you track expenses, create budgets, and set financial goals.

Tips for Effective Budgeting:
Be realistic:

Your budget should be based on your actual income and expenses, not on what you wish you could afford.

Track your spending:

Monitor your spending regularly to identify areas where you can cut back or make adjustments.

Automate your savings:

Set up automatic transfers from your checking account to your savings account to ensure consistent savings.

Review your budget regularly:

Life circumstances change, so it's important to review and adjust your budget periodically.

Building Savings:

Once you have a budget in place, you can start building your savings. Saving is crucial for financial security, offering a safety net for unexpected expenses and providing a foundation for future investments.

Strategies for Effective Saving:

Emergency Fund:

Start by building an emergency fund to cover at least three to six months of essential expenses. This fund will provide a cushion for unexpected job loss, medical bills, or other emergencies.

Short-Term Savings:

Set aside funds for specific short-term goals, such as a vacation, home improvement projects, or a down payment on a car.

Long-Term Savings:

Consider saving for long-term goals such as retirement, education, or a future down payment on a home.

Managing Debt:

Debt can be a significant financial burden, impacting your ability to save and reach your goals. It's important to develop a strategy for managing debt effectively.

Debt Management Strategies:
Snowball Method:

This method focuses on paying off debts with the smallest balances first, providing a sense of accomplishment and motivation to keep going.

Avalanche Method:

This method prioritizes paying off debts with the highest interest rates first, minimizing overall interest costs over time.

Debt Consolidation:

This involves combining multiple debts into a single loan with a lower interest rate, potentially reducing monthly payments.

Negotiation:

Contact your creditors and explore the possibility of negotiating lower interest rates, payment plans, or debt forgiveness.

Building Financial Literacy:

Financial literacy is essential for making informed financial decisions. This involves understanding basic financial concepts such as budgeting, saving, investing, credit, and debt.

Resources for Enhancing Financial Literacy:

Financial Literacy Programs:

Many community organizations and government agencies offer free or low-cost financial literacy programs.

Online Resources:

Numerous websites and apps provide financial education materials, tools, and calculators.

Books and Articles:

Explore a wide range of books and articles on personal finance and investing to expand your knowledge.

Investing:

Investing your savings is a powerful way to grow your wealth over time.

Investing Basics:

Risk Tolerance:Consider your risk tolerance and investment timeline before choosing investments.

Diversification:

Spread your investments across different asset classes to minimize risk.

Long-Term Perspective:

Invest with a long-term perspective, understanding that market fluctuations are normal.

Types of Investments:

Stocks:

Shares of ownership in a company.

Bonds:

Loans to companies or governments.

Mutual Funds:

Pools of money invested in a variety of stocks, bonds, or other assets.

Exchange-Traded Funds (ETFs):

Similar to mutual funds but traded on stock exchanges.

Real Estate:

Owning property for rental income or appreciation.

Seeking Professional Advice:

Don't hesitate to seek professional guidance from a financial advisor, especially if you have complex financial needs or are unsure about investing strategies.

Remember,

Your Financial Security is Your Right.

You deserve a future free from financial control and manipulation. By setting goals, creating a budget, building savings, and developing your financial literacy, you are taking steps to reclaim your power and build a brighter financial future. As you embark on this journey, remember that **You Are Not Alone.**

There are numerous resources and support systems available to help you along the way. Seek help from trusted family members, friends, community organizations, or financial professionals. Your resilience, determination, and belief in yourself are the strongest assets you possess. Trust in your ability to overcome past challenges and create a secure and fulfilling future.

CHAPTER TWENTY SIX
Inspiring Journeys To Independence

The stories of individuals who have successfully escaped financial abuse and rebuilt their lives are powerful testaments to the resilience and strength of the human spirit.

These journeys are not always easy, often marked by hardship, setbacks, and moments of despair. But through determination, support, and a refusal to give up, they have found their way back to financial independence and emotional wellbeing.

One such story is that of Sarah, a young woman who found herself trapped in a financially abusive relationship with her partner, Mark. Mark controlled all their finances, limiting Sarah's access to money and forcing her to rely on him for every penny. He used guilt trips and threats to keep her financially dependent, making her feel powerless and isolated.

Sarah's life was a constant struggle to make ends meet. She couldn't afford to pursue her education or career aspirations, and her dreams of a brighter future seemed distant and unattainable. Mark's financial control extended beyond money, extending to her time and freedom. She was forbidden from working or socializing with friends, making her increasingly isolated and reliant on him for everything.

The turning point for Sarah came when she finally reached out to a domestic violence shelter for help. She found a safe haven where she could start to heal and rebuild her life. The shelter staff helped her understand the dynamics of financial abuse, providing her with resources and support to regain her financial independence.

Sarah was initially scared and overwhelmed by the prospect of managing her own finances, but with the support of the shelter staff, she slowly began to regain control. She enrolled in a financial literacy program, learned budgeting skills, and started exploring job opportunities.

The road to independence was not without its challenges. Sarah had to overcome her fear of taking on financial responsibility, and she faced discrimination from potential employers who doubted her abilities.

However, she persevered, fueled by a strong desire to create a better life for herself.

After months of hard work and determination, Sarah secured a job at a local bookstore. The income was modest, but it gave her a sense of freedom and accomplishment. She began to pay off her debts and slowly build a financial buffer for the future.

Sarah's journey is a powerful reminder that even in the darkest of times, hope can bloom. It illustrates that even in the face of financial abuse, it is possible to break free, rebuild, and create a brighter future.

Another inspiring story is that of David, a man who endured years of financial abuse at the hands of his wife, Emily. Emily controlled their shared finances, denying David access to money and making him feel like a financial burden. She constantly criticized his spending habits, belittled his financial contributions, and made him feel inadequate.

David was deeply ashamed of his situation. He felt trapped, unable to escape the financial control that Emily exerted over him. The shame and guilt he carried kept him silent for years, afraid of what people would think and worried about the potential consequences of speaking out. One day, David stumbled upon a support group for men experiencing domestic violence. There, he found a safe space to talk about his experiences, sharing his story with others who understood. He learned that he wasn't alone, that financial abuse could happen to men as well, and that he wasn't to blame for his situation.

The support group provided David with the courage and motivation to take action. He began to seek help from legal and financial professionals, taking steps to separate his finances from Emily's. He learned to track his expenses, budget effectively, and manage his finances independently.

The process of rebuilding his financial independence was challenging, but David's determination and resilience ultimately led him to freedom. He found a new job that allowed him to control his income and make financial decisions for himself. He started taking steps to rebuild his credit and financial security, taking control of his financial future.

David's story shows that financial abuse can happen to anyone, regardless of gender. It also highlights the importance of seeking support and building a network of allies who can help you navigate the complexities of escaping financial control.

The stories of Sarah and David are just two examples of the many individuals who have successfully escaped financial abuse and rebuilt their lives. These journeys are not always easy, but they are possible. By learning from their experiences and drawing inspiration from their resilience, we can empower ourselves to break free from financial control and reclaim our financial independence. The stories of survivors often reveal common challenges they faced and overcame. One of the most significant hurdles is the fear of leaving the abuser. Victims often feel trapped, fearing for their safety and financial security. The abuser may use threats, intimidation, or emotional manipulation to keep their victim dependent and afraid.

Many survivors also struggle with feelings of shame and guilt. They may blame themselves for the financial abuse, believing that they could have done something to prevent it. This self-blame can make it difficult to seek help or to believe that they deserve to be financially independent.

Another common challenge is the lack of access to resources and support. Many victims lack the financial resources to leave an abusive relationship, and they may not know where to turn for help. They may also be hesitant to disclose their situation for fear of judgment or disbelief.

However, despite these challenges, survivors often find ways to overcome them. They tap into their inner strength and resilience, finding the courage to leave the abusive relationship and rebuild their lives. They seek support from trusted family and friends, community organizations, legal aid, and financial experts.

Survivors also develop coping mechanisms and strategies for managing the emotional and financial challenges they face. They learn to set boundaries, prioritize their own well-being, and build their confidence.

The stories of survivors offer powerful lessons in resilience and strength. They demonstrate that even in the face of adversity, it is possible to overcome the challenges of financial abuse and build a fulfilling and independent life.

Survivors often provide valuable advice and encouragement to those currently experiencing financial abuse. They emphasize the importance of seeking help, believing in oneself, and understanding that financial independence is possible. They share their own experiences and insights, offering practical advice and emotional support to help others escape the cycle of abuse.

Survivors often emphasize the importance of building a community of support. They highlight the power of connecting with others who understand their experiences, sharing their stories and offering each other encouragement and support. This sense of community can provide victims with the strength and motivation to take action and rebuild their lives.

The journey to financial independence is not a linear path. It involves overcoming fear, building confidence, and navigating a complex system of resources and support. It is essential to acknowledge that financial abuse is a form of violence, and victims deserve support and resources to rebuild their lives.

The stories of survivors are powerful reminders that financial abuse is a real and devastating issue. By sharing their experiences, they shed light on this hidden form of domestic violence and empower others to seek help and build a brighter future.

CHAPTER TWENTY SEVEN

Challenges Faced And Overcome

The journey to escaping financial abuse is rarely smooth. It's a path riddled with obstacles, each one a testament to the insidious nature of the control the abuser has exerted. These challenges are multifaceted, often a combination of emotional, psychological, and practical hurdles. Yet, amidst the pain and fear, survivors display remarkable resilience, their courage a beacon of hope for those still trapped in the cycle of abuse.

One of the most common challenges survivors face is the ***fear of retaliation*** The threat of violence, whether physical, emotional, or financial, often hangs heavy over their heads. This fear can paralyze them, making it difficult to take steps towards independence. They may worry that leaving will trigger a violent outburst from the abuser, or that they will be financially cut off. This fear can be amplified if the abuser has threatened to harm them or their children, or if they have witnessed violence in the past.

Breaking the silence

can also be a daunting challenge. Many victims feel isolated and ashamed, believing that they are alone in their struggles. This can be exacerbated by the abuser's tactics of isolating them from friends and family, limiting their access to communication, and undermining their sense of self-worth. They may fear judgment or disbelief, making them reluctant to confide in others. This fear can be particularly pronounced when the abuse is hidden behind a facade of normalcy, making it difficult for outsiders to recognize the severity of the situation.

Navigating the legal system

can also be a significant challenge. Victims of financial abuse may face complex legal battles, struggling to prove their claims and obtain justice.

This can be a long, arduous process, often requiring legal representation, which can be costly and difficult to afford. The legal system may be slow to recognize financial abuse as a form of domestic violence, leading to frustrations and delays in obtaining protection orders or other necessary legal remedies.

Financial instability

is another formidable obstacle. The abuser may have deliberately depleted the victim's finances, leaving them with limited resources to start anew.

This can lead to feelings of helplessness and hopelessness, making it seem impossible to rebuild their lives. They may have to rely on the abuser for essential needs, creating a dangerous dependency that perpetuates the cycle of abuse.

Many survivors grapple with ***deep-seated emotional wounds*** left by the abuse. These wounds can manifest in various ways, including low self- esteem, anxiety, depression, and post-traumatic stress disorder. They may feel guilt, shame, or blame themselves for the abuse, making it difficult to move forward. The emotional toll of financial abuse can be overwhelming, hindering their ability to focus on their recovery and financial independence.

While these challenges are daunting, it is important to

remember that countless survivors have overcome them and rebuilt their lives. They have tapped into a wellspring of courage and strength, finding ways to break free from the shackles of financial control. Here are some common strategies they have employed:

Seeking Support:

Survivors have realized the importance of building a supportive network. They reach out to trusted friends, family members, support groups, and organizations dedicated to helping victims of domestic violence. This network provides emotional validation, practical assistance, and a sense of community, fostering a sense of hope and resilience.

Developing a Financial Plan:

With the support of financial advisors, counselors, and resource organizations, survivors create a comprehensive financial plan. They assess their financial situation, develop a budget, and explore options for securing financial stability. This plan might include obtaining employment, accessing government benefits, or pursuing education or vocational training to enhance their earning potential.

Reclaiming their Identity:

Recognizing the abuser's attempts to erode their sense of self-worth, survivors actively work on reclaiming their identity. They engage in activities that bring them joy, reconnect with their passions, and rebuild their self-esteem. This process might involve therapy, journaling, creative expression, or spending time with supportive loved ones.

Seeking Legal Protection:

Survivors utilize the legal system to protect themselves from further abuse. They seek restraining orders to prevent contact with the abuser, pursue legal remedies for financial abuse, and seek custody arrangements that prioritize their safety and well-being.

Focusing on Emotional Healing:

Survivors prioritize their emotional well-being by seeking professional therapy or counseling. They address the underlying emotional wounds left by the abuse, processing their experiences and developing coping mechanisms to manage the trauma. This healing journey is crucial for rebuilding self-esteem, fostering resilience, and moving forward with their lives.

Their stories are not simply tales of hardship, but testaments to human spirit. They inspire us with their courage, reminding us that even in the darkest of times, hope and resilience can prevail. They demonstrate that breaking free from financial abuse is possible, even when the odds seem stacked against them. Their triumphs illuminate the path for others, serving as a beacon of light for those still trapped in the shadows of financial control.

While each individual's journey is unique, there are common threads woven through their stories. These threads provide valuable insights into the challenges faced by survivors and the strategies they have employed to overcome them. Their experiences offer a roadmap, a reminder that healing, freedom, and financial independence are within reach. Their stories serve as a powerful reminder that no one should have to live in the shadows of financial abuse, and that support, hope, and recovery are always available.

CHAPTER TWENTY EIGHT
Lessons In Resilience And Strength

The stories of survivors of financial abuse are testaments to the incredible resilience and strength that the human spirit possesses. Each individual's journey is unique, but a common thread weaves through them all: the unwavering determination to break free from the shackles of control and rebuild their lives.

These survivors are not just victims; they are warriors who have fought invisible battles, faced unimaginable challenges, and emerged victorious. Their stories are filled with courage, perseverance, and hope. They remind us that even in the darkest of times, when financial abuse has stripped away a person's sense of self-worth and independence, the capacity for healing and growth remains.

One such story is that of Sarah, a woman who spent years trapped in a relationship with a controlling and manipulative partner. Her abuser meticulously monitored her finances, restricting her access to money and preventing her from pursuing her education and career goals. He used guilt, shame, and threats to keep her compliant, leaving her feeling isolated and powerless.

Sarah's journey to freedom was long and arduous. It involved navigating complex legal battles, rebuilding her shattered credit, and confronting the psychological scars of abuse. However, she refused to be defined by her past. With unwavering determination, she enrolled in a financial literacy program, sought support from a therapist, and created a detailed financial plan. Slowly but surely, Sarah began to reclaim her life and her financial independence.

Her story highlights the profound impact that financial abuse can have on a person's life, but it also demonstrates the incredible strength and resilience that individuals possess. Sarah's journey is a beacon of hope, proving that even in the face of seemingly insurmountable obstacles, it is possible to break free, heal, and build a brighter future.

Another powerful example is the story of David, a man who was subjected to financial abuse by his spouse. In their relationship, his wife controlled all aspects of their finances, leaving him with no access to their shared resources. David's sense of self-worth was eroded, and he began to feel trapped and helpless. He feared the consequences of speaking out or attempting to assert himself, believing that he would be left alone and destitute.

David's awakening came when he attended a support group for men who had experienced domestic violence. He realized that he wasn't alone and that his situation wasn't his fault. He found solace in the shared experiences of other men and learned strategies for regaining control of his finances.

With the support of the group and a dedicated counselor, David began to understand the dynamics of financial abuse and how it had impacted his life. He learned to identify the manipulative tactics his wife employed and to challenge her control. It was a long and difficult process, but through resilience and determination, David was able to break free from the cycle of abuse and regain his financial independence.

David's story underscores the importance of seeking support and building a network of allies. It also demonstrates that financial abuse can affect anyone, regardless of gender. It is essential to recognize that men can be victims of financial abuse, and they deserve to be heard and supported.

Financial abuse often leaves deep emotional scars, creating a sense of shame, guilt, and self-blame. It can be incredibly challenging for survivors to move past these feelings and rebuild their lives. The journey to healing is not always linear; it is a process that involves confronting painful memories, rebuilding self-esteem, and learning to trust again.

Survivors often experience feelings of vulnerability, anxiety, and fear, particularly when dealing with financial matters. They may struggle with making independent decisions, believing that they are incapable or unworthy of financial control. It is crucial to recognize and validate these emotions, offering empathy and understanding as survivors navigate this complex terrain.

The stories of Sarah and David, along with countless others, provide invaluable lessons in resilience and strength. They remind us that even in the darkest of times, when hope seems lost, the human spirit possesses the incredible ability to heal, grow, and thrive. Survivors demonstrate that financial abuse is not a sentence, but a challenge that can be overcome with the right support and determination.

Their journeys offer hope and inspiration to others who are currently experiencing financial abuse. It is essential to communicate to these individuals that they are not alone, that their experiences are valid, and that there is help available. By sharing the stories of survivors, we can empower victims to recognize the abuse they are experiencing, seek support, and ultimately break free from the cycle of financial control.

Beyond individual stories, the collective experience of survivors offers valuable insights into the strategies and techniques that have proven effective in overcoming financial abuse. These insights can guide others on their own paths to recovery and independence.

For instance, survivors often emphasize the importance of building a strong support system. This system can encompass family, friends, therapists, financial advisors, legal professionals, and support groups. It is vital to create a network of individuals who can provide emotional support, practical guidance, and a safe space for processing and sharing experiences.

Survivors also highlight the importance of financial education and literacy. Understanding financial principles, budgeting strategies, and credit management can empower individuals to regain control of their finances and build a secure future. Financial literacy programs, workshops, and online resources can provide valuable knowledge and tools for navigating financial independence.

Building self-confidence and self-esteem is another crucial aspect of the recovery process. Financial abuse often erodes a person's sense of self- worth, leaving them feeling powerless and dependent. It is important for survivors to engage in activities that rebuild their confidence and reinforce their intrinsic value.

These may include pursuing hobbies, engaging in creative pursuits, connecting with supportive communities, and setting and achieving personal goals. Rebuilding a strong sense of self is essential for breaking free from the cycle of abuse and reclaiming a sense of agency in all aspects of life, including finances.

Finally, survivors often stress the importance of seeking professional support. Therapists can provide a safe space to process the emotional trauma of financial abuse, work through feelings of guilt and shame, and develop coping mechanisms for managing the psychological impact.

Financial advisors can offer expert guidance on managing finances, developing financial plans, and rebuilding credit after abuse.

Legal professionals can provide information about legal rights and protections, assist in securing financial resources, and advocate for fair treatment in financial matters. Support groups offer a sense of community and shared understanding, providing a safe space to connect with others who have experienced similar challenges.

The stories of survivors of financial abuse are not simply narratives of pain and hardship; they are testaments to the human spirit's indomitable resilience. They offer hope, guidance, and a powerful reminder that even in the darkest of times, it is possible to break free, heal, and rebuild a life filled with strength, independence, and self-worth.

CHAPTER TWENTY NINE

Advice From Survivors To Victims

The voices of survivors carry immense power. Their stories, their struggles, and their triumphs offer a beacon of hope and a roadmap for navigating the treacherous terrain of financial abuse. They remind us that healing and recovery are possible, that the darkness can be overcome, and that a future free from financial control is within reach.

Here, in their own words, are some of the most valuable lessons and practical advice from those who have walked this path before you:

Believe in yourself.

"The most crucial piece of advice I can give is to believe in yourself," says Maria, a survivor who endured years of financial abuse. "Your abuser may have chipped away at your self-worth, but you are capable and deserving of a life where you are in control of your own finances."

Recognize the signs.

"I didn't realize I was being financially abused until it was too late," admits John, a survivor who lost everything to his manipulative partner. "Be vigilant. Look for patterns of control and manipulation. If something feels off, trust your instincts."

Seek support.

"Don't try to go through this alone," urges Sarah, who found solace and strength in connecting with other survivors. "Reach out to trusted friends, family members, or support groups. Sharing your experience can help you feel less isolated and validate your feelings."

Create a safety plan.

"Having a plan in place made all the difference for me," shares David, who successfully escaped financial abuse and built a new life for himself.

"Start small, set realistic goals, and remember that progress is progress, no matter how slow it seems."

Don't be afraid to leave.

"The fear of losing everything kept me trapped for far too long," confesses Emily, who finally mustered the courage to leave her abusive relationship. "But the truth is, staying puts you at risk of losing even more."

You are not alone.

"It's easy to feel like you're the only one going through this," says Lisa, who found comfort in the shared experiences of other survivors. "But you are not alone. There are countless people who have been where you are, and there are resources available to help you find your way out."

The path to reclaiming your financial independence may be long and arduous, but it is possible. By learning from the experiences of others, acknowledging your own strength, and seeking support, you can break free from the chains of financial abuse and build a brighter future.

These are just a few of the countless voices that rise above the silence. Their stories remind us that resilience is not a passive state, it is a journey of finding strength within ourselves, even when the world feels like it's pushing us down.

Let their words inspire you, empower you, and remind you that you are not alone. There is hope, there is strength, and there is a way out.

The Power of Community:

The journey of healing from financial abuse is often strengthened by the presence of a supportive community. A network of caring individuals – friends, family, support groups, therapists – can provide the emotional, practical, and financial assistance needed to rebuild lives. Survivors often describe the invaluable role that communities play in their recovery:

Sharing stories and finding validation:

The act of sharing one's experience with others who understand can be immensely therapeutic. Connecting with fellow survivors, whether in person or online, allows victims to validate their own feelings and realize that they are not alone in their struggles.

Gaining practical advice and strategies:

Communities offer a wealth of knowledge and shared experience. Survivors can learn from each other's successes and failures, gaining practical advice and strategies for rebuilding their lives.

Building a sense of hope and belonging:

The knowledge that you are not alone in your journey can provide an essential sense of hope and belonging. Knowing that others have overcome similar challenges can inspire resilience and motivate survivors to keep moving forward.

Building Your Support Network:

If you are currently experiencing financial abuse, or have been in the past, building a strong support network is crucial.Here are some ways to find your community:

Reach out to trusted friends and family:

While not everyone will understand or believe your experience, there are likely individuals in your life who can provide support and a listening ear. Don't hesitate to lean on those who you trust.

Seek professional help:

Therapists and counselors can provide guidance and support in navigating the emotional complexities of financial abuse.

Join support groups:

Support groups for survivors of domestic violence offer a safe and welcoming space to share your experiences, connect with others who understand, and learn from each other's journeys.

Connect online:

Many online platforms and communities provide support and resources for survivors of financial abuse.

Seek legal assistance:

An attorney can help you understand your legal rights and explore options for protecting yourself and your finances. Remember, you are not alone. Building a supportive community can be an essential step in your journey to healing and financial independence.

CHAPTER THIRTY

Building A Community Of Support

The power of community and peer support in overcoming financial abuse cannot be overstated. It's like climbing a mountain; the journey is much easier when you have others beside you to encourage, guide, and share the load. This is especially true for survivors of financial abuse, who often feel isolated, ashamed, and unsure of where to turn. Finding a community that understands your situation and provides a safe space to heal and grow is essential.

Imagine a woman named Sarah, who, after escaping an abusive relationship, felt lost and alone. Her abuser had controlled all their finances, leaving her with little to no financial knowledge or resources. Sarah struggled with anxiety and fear, unsure how she would rebuild her life. But then, she stumbled upon a support group for survivors of domestic violence.

Within this group, Sarah found a haven. She connected with other women who had experienced similar forms of abuse, sharing their stories, anxieties, and triumphs. This sense of shared understanding brought immense relief and validation. They discussed their experiences, offering practical advice and emotional support. They learned about budgeting, financial literacy, and accessing resources together, empowering each other to reclaim control of their finances.

This shared experience allowed Sarah to realize that she wasn't alone. She was part of a community that understood the complexities of her situation. The group provided a platform for her to grieve, heal, and rediscover her own strength. She found guidance in navigating legal systems, rebuilding her credit, and securing housing. The shared journeys of the women in the group helped Sarah to see that healing was possible, and that a life free from financial abuse was within reach.

The impact of a supportive community can be profound. It provides:

1. A Safe Space to Share and Heal:

Survivors often feel overwhelmed by shame, fear, and isolation. A supportive community provides a safe space to speak openly and honestly about their experiences without judgment. Sharing their stories can be a powerful step in the healing process, allowing them to reclaim their narrative and regain a sense of control.

2. Validation and Understanding:

The experience of financial abuse can be incredibly isolating and difficult to comprehend for those who haven't lived through it. A community of survivors offers validation and understanding. Knowing that others have gone through similar challenges provides a sense of belonging and reduces the feelings of isolation.

3. Practical Support and Guidance:

Support groups can offer practical advice on navigating legal systems, accessing resources, and rebuilding finances. Members often share their own experiences, offering tips and strategies based on what worked for them. This peer-to-peer knowledge sharing can be invaluable in empowering survivors to take charge of their financial future.

4. Building a Network of Trust:

Trust is often shattered in financially abusive relationships. Building a network of trust with other survivors can be a crucial step in moving forward. The support group becomes a safe haven where survivors can build strong and supportive relationships with individuals who understand their journey.

5. Empowerment and Resilience:

Being surrounded by other survivors who have overcome similar challenges can foster a sense of empowerment. Witnessing their resilience and strength can inspire survivors to believe in their own capacity to heal and rebuild their lives. The collective strength of the community becomes a driving force for positive change.

Beyond Support Groups:

While support groups are invaluable, there are many other ways to build a community of support. Here are some ideas:

1. Connect with Local Organizations:

Many organizations dedicated to domestic violence prevention and survivor support offer a variety of programs and resources, including support groups, counseling,legal aid, and financial assistance. Reaching out to these organizations can connect you with a network of professionals and other survivors.

2. Reach Out to Family and Friends:

While some family and friends may not fully understand the complexities of financial abuse, others may be willing to listen and offer support.

Openly communicating your needs and seeking their understanding can create a stronger bond and provide a valuable source of emotional support.

3. Online Communities:

Several online forums, groups, and websites dedicated to financial abuse survivors provide a virtual space for sharing experiences, seeking advice, and connecting with others. These platforms can be particularly helpful for survivors who feel isolated or unable to attend in-person meetings.

4. Seek Professional Help:

Therapy and counseling can be invaluable in processing the emotional impact of financial abuse. A therapist can provide a safe and confidential space to work through trauma, develop coping mechanisms, and build self- esteem.

Building a community of support is not a one-time event, but an ongoing process. It involves actively seeking out connections, sharing your experiences, and building trust with others. Remember, you are not alone in this journey. There are people who understand, care, and are ready to help you reclaim your financial freedom and rebuild your life.

Real-Life Examples:

Maria:

Maria, a single mother, experienced years of financial abuse at the hands of her partner. He controlled all their finances, leaving her with no access to money or resources. After leaving him, she felt lost and overwhelmed. But through a local women's shelter, she connected with a financial literacy program and a support group for survivors. The program taught her about budgeting, saving, and accessing credit. The support group provided a safe space to share her struggles and receive encouragement. Maria gradually rebuilt her financial independence, secured stable housing, and created a brighter future for herself and her children.

David:

David was a victim of financial abuse at the hands of his spouse, who had emptied their joint accounts and left him with mounting debt. He felt deeply ashamed and isolated. But after finding an online forum for survivors of financial abuse, he realized he wasn't alone. He connected with other men who had experienced similar situations. Through the forum, David received advice on negotiating with creditors, seeking legal assistance, and rebuilding his credit. The online community provided him with the validation and support he needed to reclaim his financial stability.

Lisa:

Lisa, a young woman who had recently left an abusive relationship, struggled with fear and anxiety about managing her finances independently. Her abuser had controlled all their finances, leaving her with no knowledge or experience. Through a support group for survivors of domestic violence, Lisa met other women who had faced similar challenges. They shared practical advice on budgeting, setting up bank accounts, and creating a financial plan. The group helped Lisa gain the confidence and skills she needed to manage her finances effectively and build a secure future for herself.

These are just a few examples of how community and peer support have played a vital role in helping survivors of financial abuse reclaim their lives. It is a powerful testament to the strength and resilience that can arise from shared experiences, understanding, and support.

CHAPTER THIRTY ONE

Identifying Available Resources

The journey to escaping financial abuse isn't just about breaking free from a controlling partner; it's about reclaiming your power and building a secure future. This chapter will serve as your guide to the resources and support systems available to help you navigate this challenging path.

Imagine yourself standing at a crossroads, the weight of financial abuse still heavy on your shoulders. You may feel lost and uncertain, but know that you are not alone. You have a right to financial freedom and security, and there are countless resources out there ready to empower you.

Understanding Your Options

The first step is to understand the vast network of support systems available to you. Think of it as a toolbox filled with essential tools to help you regain control of your finances. These resources can be categorized into several key areas, each offering a specific set of tools to aid your recovery:

1. Financial Support and Guidance:
Financial Advisors:

Financial advisors can provide personalized guidance on managing your finances, creating budgets, and developing long-term financial strategies. They can help you understand complex financial concepts and navigate the world of investments and savings. Look for advisors who specialize in domestic violence situations and understand the unique challenges you may face.

Credit Counseling Agencies:

These agencies offer free or low-cost counseling to help you manage debt, improve your credit score, and develop a budget. They can also provide guidance on dealing with financial institutions and disputing unfair credit reporting.

Government Assistance Programs:

The government offers a variety of financial assistance programs, including food stamps (SNAP), housing assistance (Section 8), and medical assistance (Medicaid). These programs can provide temporary relief and help you stabilize your finances.

Community Development Financial Institutions (CDFIs):

CDFIs are non-profit organizations that provide financial services to low- and moderate-income communities. They often offer affordable loans, financial education, and other resources that can help you build financial stability.

2. Legal and Advocacy Services:
Legal Aid Organizations:

Legal aid organizations provide free or low-cost legal assistance to individuals who cannot afford an attorney. They can help you understand your legal rights, navigate the legal system, and seek protection orders against your abuser.

Domestic Violence Shelters and Advocates:

Shelters provide a safe haven for victims of domestic violence and can offer legal advocacy, counseling, and resources to help you rebuild your life.

Pro Bono Attorneys:

Some attorneys offer their services pro bono (free of charge) to individuals who cannot afford legal representation. You can search for pro bono lawyers through legal aid organizations or online directories.

3. Mental Health and Emotional Support:
Therapy and Counseling:

Therapy and counseling can provide you with a safe space to process your experiences, work through emotional trauma, and develop coping mechanisms. Therapists specializing in domestic violence can provide support and guidance tailored to your specific needs.

Support Groups:

Support groups connect you with others who have experienced similar situations, providing a sense of community, understanding, and shared strength. These groups can offer practical advice, emotional support, and a sense of hope.

Crisis Hotlines:

Crisis hotlines offer immediate support and resources to victims of domestic violence 24/7. They can provide you with information about local services, shelter options, and safety planning.

4. Online Resources and Tools:
Financial Literacy Websites and Blogs:

Many online resources offer free financial education and tools, including budgeting calculators, debt management resources, and tips for saving money.

Financial Empowerment Apps:

Mobile apps can help you track your spending, create budgets, and manage your finances on the go.

Online Support Communities:

Online forums and support groups offer a space for victims to share their experiences, seek advice, and build a virtual community.

Building Your Support System

The resources listed above are just a starting point. Building a strong support system is crucial to your journey toward financial freedom and independence.

Here's how to create a personalized support network: Reach out to trusted friends and family members:

Share your experiences with people you trust and who can provide emotional support, practical assistance, or financial help.

Connect with community organizations and support groups:

Attend support group meetings or join online communities to connect with other survivors and share experiences.

Seek professional help:

Don't hesitate to reach out to therapists, counselors, or legal experts for guidance and support.

Develop a safety plan:

Create a plan for how you will stay safe if your abuser tries to control or manipulate you financially. This might include changing your bank accounts, setting up separate credit cards, or securing your financial documents.

Remember, you are not alone in this journey. There are people who care about you and want to help. Reach out for support, empower yourself with knowledge, and take steps to reclaim your financial freedom and security.

CHAPTER THIRTY TWO

Connecting With Financial Advisors And Legal Experts

The road to financial independence after experiencing financial abuse can be daunting, but it doesn't have to be a solo journey. Seeking professional guidance from financial advisors and legal experts can be invaluable in navigating the complexities of rebuilding your finances and protecting your future. These professionals provide specialized knowledge and support, empowering you to make informed decisions and regain control of your financial life.

Finding the Right Financial Advisor:
Know Your Needs:

Before embarking on the search, it's crucial to understand your specific financial goals and circumstances. Are you seeking advice on budgeting, debt management, investing, or saving for the future?

Types of Financial Advisors:

Familiarize yourself with the different types of financial advisors:

Certified Financial Planner (CFP):

Holds a certification from the Certified Financial Planner Board of Standards, signifying a rigorous education and experience in financial planning.

Registered Investment Advisor (RIA):

A fiduciary who is legally obligated to act in your best interest. RIAs are required to register with the Securities and Exchange Commission (SEC) or a state regulator.

Broker-Dealers:

Primarily focus on selling securities, but they can also offer financial advice.

Fee-Only Financial Planners:

Charge fees for their services, which are typically based on a percentage of assets under management or an hourly rate.

Fee-Based Financial Planners:

May charge both fees and commissions.

Consider Your Budget:

Financial advisors vary in their fees and services. Consider your budget and select an advisor who offers a transparent fee structure and whose services align with your needs.

Vetting Potential Advisors:
Referrals:

Ask friends, family, or trusted professionals for recommendations.

Online Resources:

Websites like the Financial Planning Association (FPA), the National Association of Personal Financial Advisors (NAPFA), and the Certified Financial Planner Board of Standards (CFP Board) offer databases of certified financial advisors.

Check Credentials:

Ensure the advisor is registered and licensed in your state. Verify their credentials and experience through professional associations and regulatory bodies.

Interviews:

Schedule interviews with several potential advisors to discuss your financial goals, their services, and their approach. Be sure to ask about their experience with clients who have experienced financial abuse.

Building Trust:

A strong relationship built on trust is essential. Choose an advisor who listens attentively, communicates openly, and respects your decisions.

Working with a Financial Advisor:
Clear Communication:

Clearly articulate your financial goals, concerns, and any past experiences with financial abuse.

Transparency:

Be honest and transparent with your financial situation, including any

debts, assets, and income sources.

Active Participation:

Don't be afraid to ask questions and seek clarification on any strategies or recommendations. Financial planning is a collaborative process, and you have the right to understand every step.

Financial Freedom:

Remember that you have the right to terminate the relationship with a financial advisor at any time if you are dissatisfied with their services or approach.

Seeking Legal Guidance:
Types of Legal Professionals:

Several legal professionals can assist you in navigating financial abuse:

Family Law Attorney:

Specializes in legal issues related to domestic violence, divorce, child custody, and property division.

Civil Litigation Attorney:

Handles lawsuits involving financial matters, such as fraud, breach of contract, and asset recovery.

Criminal Defense Attorney:

Represents individuals facing criminal charges related to financial abuse.

Understanding Legal Options:

Discuss your situation with an attorney to understand your legal rights and options, including:

Protective Orders:

A court order to protect you from further abuse, including financial abuse.

Asset Protection:

Legal strategies to protect your assets from being seized or misused by an abuser.

Divorce and Property Division:

Fairly dividing assets and debts in a divorce or separation.

Criminal Charges:

Pursuing criminal charges against an abuser for financial crimes.

Navigating Legal Processes:

An attorney can guide you through the complexities of legal proceedings, including:

Court Filings:

Preparing and filing necessary documents with the court.

Negotiations:

Representing you in negotiations with an abuser or their legal counsel.

Litigation:

Preparing and presenting your case in court.

Legal Aid Resources:

If you cannot afford an attorney, consider exploring legal aid resources in your area, such as:

Legal Aid Societies:

Provide free or low-cost legal services to low-income individuals.

Pro Bono Programs:

Connect volunteer attorneys with those in need of legal assistance.

Government Legal Assistance Programs:

Offered by state and local governments.

Building a Strong Team:
Collaboration:

Working with a financial advisor and a legal expert can create a strong support system to help you navigate the challenges of rebuilding your financial life.

Clear Communication:

Open and clear communication between your financial advisor, attorney, and yourself is essential.

Shared Goals:

Ensure that your advisor and attorney understand your financial goals and legal objectives.

Trust and Empowerment:

Choose professionals who you trust and who empower you to take control of your financial future.

Empowering Yourself:
Information is Power:

Educate yourself about financial abuse, your rights, and the resources available to you.

Seek Support:

Don't hesitate to reach out for support from friends, family, support groups, or therapists.

Believe in Yourself:

You are not alone in your journey to financial independence. Believe in your ability to rebuild your life and reclaim your financial security.

The path to recovery from financial abuse is often long and challenging, but with the right support system and a commitment to your own empowerment, you can build a brighter financial future. Seek guidance from financial advisors and legal experts to navigate the complexities, protect your interests, and regain control of your financial well-being. Remember, you deserve financial freedom and security.

CHAPTER THIRTY THREE

Community Organizations And Support Groups

The journey of escaping financial abuse often feels overwhelming, but you are not alone. There is a network of support available to help you reclaim your financial independence and rebuild your life. This chapter will explore the various resources and support systems that can guide you on your path to healing and empowerment.

Community Organizations and Support Groups

One of the most crucial steps in your recovery is connecting with organizations and support groups dedicated to assisting victims of domestic violence and financial abuse. These groups offer a safe and understanding space to share your experiences, access vital resources, and gain strength from others who have walked a similar path. National Domestic Violence Hotline

The National Domestic Violence Hotline (1-800-799-SAFE) provides confidential support and resources for survivors of domestic violence, including financial abuse. Their trained advocates are available 24/7 to offer immediate assistance, information on local shelters, legal aid, and other resources. They can also provide referrals to financial literacy programs and counseling services.

The National Coalition Against Domestic Violence (NCADV)

NCADV is a leading organization advocating for survivors of domestic violence. They provide a comprehensive range of resources, including information on financial abuse, legal advocacy, and support services. Their website offers a wealth of materials, including fact sheets, articles, and videos explaining the dynamics of financial abuse and strategies for recovery.

The National Network to End Domestic Violence (NNEDV)

NNEDV is a network of domestic violence programs nationwide. They provide information, resources, and training to organizations and individuals working to end domestic violence. Their website offers a directory of local domestic violence programs, including those specializing in financial abuse, where you can access support and resources tailored to your specific needs.

The National Financial Educators Council (NFEC)

The NFEC is a non-profit organization dedicated to promoting financial literacy and empowerment. They offer various resources, including educational materials, workshops, and online tools that can help survivors of financial abuse rebuild their financial skills and independence. Their website offers a wealth of information on budgeting, credit management, and financial planning,which can be particularly useful for individuals who have been financially controlled or exploited. Local Domestic Violence Shelters and Programs.

Many communities have local domestic violence shelters and programs that offer a wide range of services to survivors, including emergency housing, counseling, legal assistance, and financial support. These programs are often staffed by experienced professionals who can provide guidance and resources specific to your situation. Support Groups for Survivors.

Joining a support group for survivors of domestic violence can be incredibly empowering.. These groups allow you to connect with others who understand your experiences and offer a safe space to share your story, receive encouragement, and learn from each other's journeys. Support groups can provide a sense of community and belonging, helping you feel less isolated and alone in your healing process. Financial Counseling Services.

Financial counselors can provide expert guidance and support to individuals who have experienced financial abuse. They can help you assess your current financial situation, develop a budget, manage debt, and plan for your financial future.

Many financial counseling services offer free or low-cost assistance to those in need. Legal Aid Organizations. Legal aid organizations can provide assistance with legal issues related to domestic violence, including financial abuse. They can help you understand your rights, navigate the legal system, and access resources for obtaining protection orders, divorce proceedings, or other legal remedies. Online Support Communities and Forums.

Online support communities and forums dedicated to survivors of domestic violence can provide a sense of connection and shared understanding.

These platforms allow you to connect with others online, share your experiences, ask questions, and receive support from those who have gone through similar challenges.

Connecting with Support Groups

Finding the right support group can make a significant difference in your healing journey. Consider the following tips for connecting with a group that aligns with your needs:

Seek recommendations:

Ask trusted friends, family members, or professionals for referrals to support groups in your area.

Check online directories:

Websites such as the National Domestic Violence Hotline, NCADV, and

NNEDV offer online directories of support groups and programs.

Contact local community centers:

Many community centers host support groups for survivors of domestic violence.

Attend local events:

Domestic violence awareness events often feature information about support groups and services available in the community.

Consider online groups:

Online support groups can be an excellent resource for connecting with individuals from different locations and backgrounds.

Benefits of Support Groups

Support groups offer a range of benefits to survivors of financial abuse, including:

A safe space to share experiences:

Sharing your story with others who understand your experience can be incredibly therapeutic.

Emotional validation and support:

Feeling understood and supported by others can help you process your emotions and build your self-esteem.

Practical advice and tips:

Members of support groups can share their experiences and offer practical advice on managing finances, rebuilding your life, and navigating the legal system.

Increased sense of community and belonging:

Connecting with others who have experienced similar challenges can help you feel less isolated and alone in your recovery.

Empowerment and motivation:

Hearing the stories of others who have overcome adversity can inspire you to take charge of your own life and build a brighter future.

Building Your Support Network

Remember that you don't have to go through this alone. Building a strong support network of trusted friends, family members, and professionals can provide you with the strength and resources you need to heal and thrive.

Reach out to loved ones:

Talk to trusted friends and family members about what you are going through. Share your experiences, seek their support, and let them know how they can help.

Connect with professionals:

Consider working with a therapist, counselor, or financial advisor who can provide expert guidance and support.

Seek legal assistance:

If you need legal assistance, contact a legal aid organization or lawyer specializing in domestic violence.

Join support groups:

Participating in support groups can help you connect with others who understand your experiences and provide a sense of community.

Remember, healing from financial abuse is a journey, and it takes time and support. Be patient with yourself, seek help when you need it, and know that you are not alone in your fight for financial independence and a brighter future. Online Platforms and Tools for Financial Empowerment

The digital age offers a wealth of resources and tools to support victims of financial abuse in regaining their financial independence. These online platforms can serve as a lifeline, providing information, support, and practical tools to navigate the complexities of financial recovery.

Financial Literacy and Education:

The internet is brimming with resources designed to boost financial literacy. Websites and online courses can help victims understand budgeting, credit management, investing, and other essential financial concepts. Platforms like Khan Academy, Investopedia, and NerdWallet offer free courses and articles covering a wide range of financial topics. These resources can equip victims with the knowledge and skills needed to make informed financial decisions and regain control of their finances.

Budgeting and Tracking Tools:

Managing finances effectively requires a solid budgeting plan and accurate tracking of expenses. Thankfully, numerous online tools simplify this process. Apps like Mint, Personal Capital, and YNAB (You Need a Budget) provide features for budgeting, expense tracking, and goal setting. These tools can help victims gain visibility into their spending habits, identify areas for savings, and develop a realistic budget that promotes financial stability.

Credit Monitoring and Repair:

Financial abuse often involves the abuser damaging the victim's credit score. Online credit monitoring services like Credit Karma, Experian, and TransUnion allow victims to monitor their credit reports for inaccuracies and potential fraud. They can also provide alerts for suspicious activity, enabling prompt action to protect their credit. Furthermore, these services often offer credit repair tools and advice to help victims rebuild their credit after abuse.

Debt Management and Consolidation:

Victims of financial abuse may find themselves burdened with debt accumulated by their abusers. Online platforms can help manage and potentially consolidate debt. Debt consolidation services like those offered by LendingTree and Credible connect individuals with lenders offering lower interest rates and more manageable repayment plans. This can significantly reduce monthly debt payments and provide a path towards financial recovery.

Legal Assistance and Advocacy:

Online legal resources can empower victims to understand their legal rights and navigate the complexities of the legal system. Websites like Legal Aid Services of America, the National Domestic Violence Hotline, and the National Coalition Against Domestic Violence provide information on laws related to financial abuse, legal remedies available, and legal assistance resources. Victims can also connect with online legal services that offer virtual consultations and legal representation for cases involving financial abuse.

Support Networks and Community Forums:

The internet fosters a sense of community and offers a platform for victims to connect with others who share their experiences. Online support groups, forums, and social media communities provide a safe space for victims to share their stories, seek advice, and find emotional support. Platforms like Reddit (r/financialabuse), Facebook groups dedicated to financial abuse, and online support forums like 7 Cups of Tea allow victims to connect with others going through similar challenges.

Financial Counseling and Support Services:

Numerous online platforms connect individuals with financial counselors and support services. Websites like the National Endowment for Financial Education (NEFE), the Financial Planning Association (FPA), and the American Institute of Certified Public Accountants (AICPA) offer directories of certified financial planners and counselors who can provide personalized guidance and support. Online financial coaching programs can also offer personalized assistance and accountability to help victims develop sustainable financial habits.

Financial Safety and Security:

Protecting financial information online is paramount after experiencing financial abuse. Online security tools like antivirus software, password managers, and two-factor authentication can enhance digital security and minimize the risk of further financial exploitation. Victims should also prioritize securing their online accounts and reviewing their financial statements regularly for any suspicious activity.

Using Online Platforms Wisely:

While online platforms offer invaluable resources and support, it's crucial to use them wisely. Be cautious of scams and phishing attempts. Verify the authenticity of websites and resources before sharing personal information. Use secure passwords and be wary of clicking suspicious links. Remember, online platforms should be viewed as a supplement to real-life support and not a replacement for professional help.

The Importance of Professional Guidance:

While online resources can provide valuable information and support, it's essential to seek professional guidance from financial advisors, legal experts, and mental health professionals. A financial advisor can create a personalized financial plan, a lawyer can help navigate legal challenges, and a therapist can address the emotional and psychological impacts of financial abuse.

Breaking the Cycle of Financial Abuse:

The internet, with its vast resources and interconnected communities, has become an invaluable tool for victims of financial abuse.

By accessing online platforms, victims can gain knowledge, access support, and develop the tools necessary to rebuild their lives and regain financial independence. However, it's crucial to remember that online resources should complement, not replace, professional guidance and real- life support. Through a combination of online resources, professional support, and personal resilience, victims can break free from the cycle of financial abuse and create a secure future. Creating a Sustainable Path Forward.

Creating a sustainable path forward necessitates a comprehensive approach that goes beyond the immediate need for safety and security. It involves developing a long-term strategy that empowers individuals to achieve financial stability and independence. This involves taking proactive steps to rebuild their financial lives, educate themselves about financial management, and secure a future free from the shackles of financial abuse.

The journey to financial independence starts with a thorough assessment of one's current financial situation. This requires taking stock of all assets, liabilities, and ongoing expenses. It's crucial to understand the extent of the damage caused by financial abuse and identify any debts or liabilities that need to be addressed. This assessment serves as a foundation for building a personalized financial plan that aligns with individual needs and aspirations.

Developing a financial escape plan is a critical step in regaining control over one's finances. This plan should outline a clear roadmap for achieving financial independence. It may include strategies for managing existing debts, rebuilding credit, securing employment, and saving for future goals. The escape plan should be tailored to individual circumstances and resources, with specific timelines and milestones to track progress.

Budgeting and managing resources effectively are essential for maintaining financial stability. It's crucial to create a realistic budget that accounts for all expenses and income sources. This involves prioritizing essential needs, such as housing, food, and healthcare, while identifying areas where spending can be reduced or eliminated. Developing sound money management habits, like tracking expenses, saving regularly, and avoiding impulsive purchases, can significantly contribute to long-term financial security.

Investing in financial literacy is a crucial step towards financial independence.

Understanding basic financial concepts, such as budgeting, saving, investing, and debt management, can empower individuals to make informed financial decisions.

There are numerous resources available, including online courses, workshops, and books, that can provide the necessary knowledge and skills.

Building a support network is essential for navigating the challenges of financial recovery. It's important to surround oneself with individuals who offer emotional support, practical advice, and a non-judgmental space to share experiences. Connecting with friends, family, support groups, or financial advisors can provide invaluable guidance and encouragement during this journey.

Reclaiming control over finances after experiencing financial abuse is a significant step towards healing and empowerment. It's crucial to remember that building financial independence is a process that requires patience, persistence, and a belief in one's ability to achieve financial security. By embracing a proactive approach, seeking support, and developing sound financial habits, individuals can break free from the cycle of financial abuse and create a sustainable path towards a brighter future.

One of the most effective ways to build a sustainable path forward is by securing stable employment. This involves exploring career options that align with individual skills, interests, and long-term goals. It may require retraining, education, or job search strategies tailored to the current job market. Finding a job that provides a livable wage, benefits, and growth opportunities is crucial for establishing financial stability.

Developing a plan for long-term financial security involves creating a savings strategy that addresses both short-term and long-term goals.

This may include saving for emergency funds, building a down payment for a home, or investing for retirement. It's important to prioritize savings and allocate a portion of income regularly towards these goals.

Investing in one's future can also involve exploring investment options that align with individual risk tolerance and financial goals. This may include diversifying investments across different asset classes, such as stocks, bonds, and real estate. Seeking advice from a reputable financial advisor can provide valuable insights and guidance on navigating the complex world of investment.

Creating a sustainable path forward also entails addressing any outstanding debts. This involves developing a debt management plan that prioritizes paying off high-interest debts while minimizing the impact on daily expenses. Utilizing tools like debt consolidation loans or credit counseling services can help streamline repayment and reduce overall debt burden.

The path to financial independence is not always linear and may encounter unexpected challenges. It's essential to develop a plan that is flexible and adaptable to changing circumstances. Regularly reviewing and adjusting financial goals, budget, and investment strategies can ensure that the plan remains relevant and effective over time.

Building financial independence is a long-term endeavor that requires commitment, discipline, and a belief in one's ability to succeed. It involves breaking free from the patterns of financial abuse, acquiring knowledge and skills, and creating a sustainable plan for the future. By embracing a proactive approach, seeking support, and cultivating a resilient mindset, individuals can reclaim their financial autonomy and build a future free from financial abuse.

CHAPTER THIRTY FOUR
Acknowledgments

Writing this book has been a deeply personal and rewarding experience. I am eternally grateful to the many individuals who have contributed their time, expertise, and unwavering support to this project.

First and foremost, I would like to express my heartfelt gratitude to the survivors of financial abuse who bravely shared their stories with me. Their resilience, strength, and willingness to speak out are truly inspiring. Your courage has given voice to a hidden form of domestic violence, and I hope this book helps empower others to break free from its clutches.

I am deeply indebted to the professionals and advocates who have dedicated their lives to combating domestic violence and supporting survivors. Your tireless work is a testament to the commitment to creating a safer and more just world.

I want to extend my sincere appreciation to the financial experts, legal professionals, and researchers who provided invaluable insights and guidance. Your knowledge and expertise have been instrumental in shaping this book.

Finally, having endured financial and domestic violence myself, I discovered that writing this book has been instrumental in healing deep- seated wounds that I had hidden due to shame and denial. Observing the bravery of others during my research, has taught me that our past experiences don't dictate our identity, and I am optimistic about a future filled with healthy relationships and financial abundance.......

Appendix

This appendix provides a comprehensive list of resources available to victims of financial abuse, including:

National Domestic Violence Hotline:

1-800-799-7233 (www.thehotline.org)

National Coalition Against Domestic Violence:

www.ncadv.org

National Network to End Domestic Violence:

www.nnedv.org **Financial Abuse Center:** www.financialabuse.org

National Financial Empowerment Center: www.nfec.org

National Consumer Law Center: www.nclc.org

Local Domestic Violence Shelters and Advocacy Organizations:

(Your local phone book or internet search can help you find these organizations)

Legal Aid Organizations:

(Local legal aid organizations can provide free or low-cost legal services)

Glossary

Coercive Control:
A pattern of behavior used to control, manipulate, and isolate a victim.

Financial Abuse:
A form of domestic violence where an abuser uses financial control to gain power and dominance over their victim.

Financial Independence:
The ability to manage one's own finances and make financial decisions independently.

Financial Safety Plan:
A plan to protect one's financial well-being and prevent further financial abuse.

Isolation:
A tactic used by abusers to limit the victim's contact with family, friends, and support systems.

Manipulation:
The use of psychological tactics to control and influence another person's behavior.

Power Imbalance:
An unequal distribution of power in a relationship, which can lead to abuse.

Resource Management:
The process of budgeting, saving, and spending money effectively.

Books By This Author

Quiet Suffering: The Tangled Web Of A Functional Addict

The world often presents us with a carefully curated facade, a mask that conceals the complexities beneath the surface. In the case of Samantha Taylor, the mask she wears is one of undeniable success. She's a young woman juggling a demanding career as a paramedic with pre-med studies, a seemingly picture-perfect marriage to her high school sweetheart, and a life that outwardly embodies the American Dream.

But beneath the surface lies a secret—a deep-seated addiction that has been consuming her since her early teens. Trauma and a need to escape reality fueled this destructive spiral, drawing her into a world of drugs and fleeting highs. Her life, once a tapestry of hope and ambition, is now woven with threads of dependency, each one a reminder of her precarious grasp on sanity.

This is a story about the dark side of addiction, a world where the line between reality and escape blurs, and the consequences of each choice can be life-altering.

Samantha's journey is one of self-destruction and redemption, a testament to the resilience of the human spirit in the face of adversity. It's a story of the invisible chains that bind us, the secrets we keep, and the choices that define our destiny.